Number 153
Spring 2017

New Directions for Evaluation

Paul R. Brandon
Editor-in-Chief

Improvement Science in Evaluation: Methods and Uses

Christina A. Christie
Moira Inkelas
Sebastian Lemire
Editors

Improvement Science in Evaluation: Methods and Uses
Christina A. Christie, Moira Inkelas, and Sebastian Lemire (eds.)
New Directions for Evaluation, no. 153
Editor-in-Chief: *Paul R. Brandon*

New Directions for Evaluation, (ISSN 1097-6736; Online ISSN: 1534-875X), is published quarterly on behalf of the American Evaluation Association by Wiley Subscription Services, Inc., a Wiley Company, 111 River St., Hoboken, NJ 07030-5774 USA.
Postmaster: Send all address changes to *New Directions for Evaluation*, John Wiley & Sons Inc., C/O The Sheridan Press, PO Box 465, Hanover, PA 17331 USA.

Information for subscribers
New Directions for Evaluation is published in 4 issues per year. Institutional subscription prices for 2017 are:
Print & Online: US$484 (US), US$538 (Canada & Mexico), US$584 (Rest of World), €381 (Europe), £304 (UK). Prices are exclusive of tax. Asia-Pacific GST, Canadian GST/HST and European VAT will be applied at the appropriate rates. For more information on current tax rates, please go to www.wileyonlinelibrary.com/tax-vat. The price includes online access to the current and all online backfiles to January 1st 2013, where available. For other pricing options, including access information and terms and conditions, please visit www.wileyonlinelibrary.com/access.

Delivery Terms and Legal Title
Where the subscription price includes print issues and delivery is to the recipient's address, delivery terms are **Delivered at Place (DAP)**; the recipient is responsible for paying any import duty or taxes. Title to all issues transfers FOB our shipping point, freight prepaid. We will endeavour to fulfil claims for missing or damaged copies within six months of publication, within our reasonable discretion and subject to availability.

Back issues: Single issues from current and recent volumes are available at the current single issue price from cs-journals@wiley.com.

Disclaimer
The Publisher, the American Evaluation Association and Editors cannot be held responsible for errors or any consequences arising from the use of information contained in this journal; the views and opinions expressed do not necessarily reflect those of the Publisher, the American Evaluation Association and Editors, neither does the publication of advertisements constitute any endorsement by the Publisher, the American Evaluation Association and Editors of the products advertised.

Publisher: New Directions for Evaluation is published by Wiley Periodicals, Inc., 350 Main St., Malden, MA 02148-5020.

Journal Customer Services: For ordering information, claims and any enquiry concerning your journal subscription please go to www.wileycustomerhelp.com/ask or contact your nearest office.
Americas: Email: cs-journals@wiley.com; Tel: +1 781 388 8598 or +1 800 835 6770 (toll free in the USA & Canada).
Europe, Middle East and Africa: Email: cs-journals@wiley.com; Tel: +44 (0) 1865 778315.
Asia Pacific: Email: cs-journals@wiley.com; Tel: +65 6511 8000.
Japan: For Japanese speaking support, Email: cs-japan@wiley.com.
Visit our Online Customer Help available in 7 languages at www.wileycustomerhelp.com/ask

Production Editor: Meghanjali Singh (email: mesingh@wiley.com).

Wiley's Corporate Citizenship initiative seeks to address the environmental, social, economic, and ethical challenges faced in our business and which are important to our diverse stakeholder groups. Since launching the initiative, we have focused on sharing our content with those in need, enhancing community philanthropy, reducing our carbon impact, creating global guidelines and best practices for paper use, establishing a vendor code of ethics, and engaging our colleagues and other stakeholders in our efforts. Follow our progress at www.wiley.com/go/citizenship

View this journal online at wileyonlinelibrary.com/journal/ev

Wiley is a founding member of the UN-backed HINARI, AGORA, and OARE initiatives. They are now collectively known as Research4Life, making online scientific content available free or at nominal cost to researchers in developing countries. Please visit Wiley's Content Access - Corporate Citizenship site: http://www.wiley.com/WileyCDA/Section/id-390082.html

Printed in the USA by The Sheridan Group.

Address for Editorial Correspondence: Editor-in-chief, Paul R. Brandon, New Directions for Evaluation, Email: brandon@hawaii.edu

Abstracting and Indexing Services
The Journal is indexed by Academic Search Alumni Edition (EBSCO Publishing); Education Research Complete (EBSCO Publishing); Higher Education Abstracts (Claremont Graduate University); SCOPUS (Elsevier); Social Services Abstracts (ProQuest); Sociological Abstracts (ProQuest); Worldwide Political Sciences Abstracts (ProQuest).

Cover design: Wiley
Cover Images: © Lava 4 images | Shutterstock

For submission instructions, subscription and all other information visit:
wileyonlinelibrary.com/journal/ev

Editorial Policy and Procedures

New Directions for Evaluation, a quarterly sourcebook, is an official publication of the American Evaluation Association. The journal publishes works on all aspects of evaluation, with an emphasis on presenting timely and thoughtful reflections on leading-edge issues of evaluation theory, practice, methods, the profession, and the organizational, cultural, and societal context within which evaluation occurs. Each issue of the journal is devoted to a single topic, with contributions solicited, organized, reviewed, and edited by one or more guest editors.

The editor-in-chief is seeking proposals for journal issues from around the globe about topics new to the journal (although topics discussed in the past can be revisited). A diversity of perspectives and creative bridges between evaluation and other disciplines, as well as chapters reporting original empirical research on evaluation, are encouraged. A wide range of topics and substantive domains are appropriate for publication, including evaluative endeavors other than program evaluation; however, the proposed topic must be of interest to a broad evaluation audience.

Journal issues may take any of several forms. Typically they are presented as a series of related chapters, but they might also be presented as a debate; an account, with critique and commentary, of an exemplary evaluation; a feature-length article followed by brief critical commentaries; or perhaps another form proposed by guest editors.

Submitted proposals must follow the format found via the Association's website at http://www.eval.org/Publications/NDE.asp. Proposals are sent to members of the journal's Editorial Advisory Board and to relevant substantive experts for single-blind peer review. The process may result in acceptance, a recommendation to revise and resubmit, or rejection. The journal does not consider or publish unsolicited single manuscripts.

Before submitting proposals, all parties are asked to contact the editor-in-chief, who is committed to working constructively with potential guest editors to help them develop acceptable proposals. For additional information about the journal, see the "Statement of the Editor-in-Chief" in the Spring 2013 issue (No. 137).

Paul R. Brandon, Editor-in-Chief
University of Hawai'i at Mānoa
College of Education
1776 University Avenue
Castle Memorial Hall, Rm. 118
Honolulu, HI 968222463
e-mail: nde@eval.org

CONTENTS

EDITORS' NOTES

E valuation is about change. As Carol Weiss reminds us, "Evaluation is a practical craft, designed to help make programs work better and to allocate resources to better programs. Evaluators expect people in authority to use evaluation results to take wise action. They take satisfaction from the chance to contribute to social betterment" (1998, p. 5). Speaking to this central purpose of evaluation, a broad range of topics related to utilization have been explored in the evaluation literature, including the conceptualization of evaluation use (Leviton & Hughes, 1981), concepts of research use (Cousins & Shulha, 2006; Hofstetter & Alkin, 2003), and empirical research on utilization (Cousins & Leithwood, 1986; Cousins & Shulha, 2006; Hofstetter & Alkin, 2003). At root, all of these contributions are about how evaluation brings about change, how evaluation contributes to social betterment.

Sharing this overarching purpose, improvement science is an approach to increasing knowledge that leads to an improvement of a product, process, or system (Moen, Nolan, & Provost, 2012). Improvement science has experienced a surge of interest over the past 30 years—especially in the health sciences. Despite the rapidly expanding reach of improvement science in education, criminal justice, and social care, among other fields, published applications of improvement science are close to nonexistent in the evaluation literature. Indeed, many evaluators know little about improvement science. What is improvement science? What does improvement science look like in real-world applications? And what might we, as evaluators, learn from the theory and practice of improvement science? These and other questions are considered in this issue of *New Directions for Evaluation*.

The primary motivation for the issue is to promote increased cross-talk and perhaps even cross-fertilization of ideas, techniques, and tools between evaluation and improvement science. Speaking directly to this aim, there are at least four areas where this cross-fertilization is particularly relevant: learning from error, examining variation, appreciating context, and focusing on systems change.

Learning from error is both friend and foe in evaluation. To be sure, the idea of trial and error can be traced back to the early ideas of social engineering (e.g., Campbell's notion of the "experimenting society") and the distinction between theory and implementation failure is a staple of theory-based evaluation. We learn from error; evaluation is no exception. That being said, the heavy focus on outcomes and fervent pursuit of "what works" have also served to depress the room for error and, in effect, any learning that results from this, in the context of many contract-funded evaluations of public programs. The error as foe is even evident in the designs

NEW DIRECTIONS FOR EVALUATION, no. 153, Spring 2017 © 2017 Wiley Periodicals, Inc., and the American Evaluation Association. Published online in Wiley Online Library (wileyonlinelibrary.com) • DOI: 10.1002/ev.20238 and methods often employed in evaluation that intentionally seek to "control," "rule out," or at least "adjust" for error. A lot of learning is potentially lost. From this perspective, improvement science offers a much-welcomed framework to carve out a learning space for error. The stepwise, piecemeal experimentation central to improvement science serves well to reduce the adverse consequences of error and allow for a progressive, trial-and-error learning.

The importance of variation has not been lost on evaluators. Most evaluators agree that programs rarely work or fail to work. Even though programs may fail on average to produce positive outcomes across many contexts, there are some contexts in which these *failed* programs actually deliver value. Programs work for some, under certain circumstances, and in constant interaction with local conditions. The sustained interest in what works for whom and under what conditions speaks to this awareness. Speaking directly to this interest in variation, improvement science offers operational guidance and concrete techniques for examining outcome variations and connecting these with program changes.

On a related point, and often as part of what explains variation in program outcomes, the complexity of the contexts in which programs are delivered is often of interest to evaluators. Evaluators work in the contexts in which problems must be understood. Because of this, evaluators encounter complex contextual issues that largely determine the success of initiatives. Evaluations that use an approach that examines program implementation and differences in success will lead to better programs because variability will be better understood. Grounded on decades of real-world applications, improvement science offers key insights on and practical guidelines for addressing the complexity of context.

Systems thinking has recently received a surge of interest among evaluators. The recognition that programs and the problems they seek to address function within broader systems is difficult to dispute. As such, it is necessary to understand the component processes of a system and how they work together, so as to understand the roots of the problem and generate innovative solutions. Sometimes quality can be improved by merely tweaking the system, that is, making small changes that enable the system to function in context the way it was designed to function. But other times the system must be redesigned from the ground up or major components changed. Motivated by systemic change, improvement science is grounded in a framework for improving systems that has been highly successful in fields as diverse as the automotive industry and health care (Kenney, 2008; Rother, 2009).

With these observations as our backdrop, the chapters in this volume address issues that are critical to both improvement science and evaluation.

Chapter 1 sets the stage by considering some of the conceptual similarities and distinctions between improvement science and evaluation. Chapter 2 provides a general introduction to the intellectual foundations, methods, and tools that collectively comprise improvement science. Chapter 3 provides the purest example of the implementation of improvement science, showcasing how iterative cycles of development and testing can provide solutions to address family- and system-level barriers to primary care. The other chapters offer illustrations of improvement science in a variety of contexts and provide illustrations of the benefits and challenges of implementing improvement science for evaluative purposes. Chapter 4 illustrates how network of diverse organizations can use iterative learning cycles to come up with promising ideas, test and prototype these ideas, and spread and sustain what is found to work for a community population. Chapter 5 describes the implementation of rapid cycles of evaluations (Plan–Do–Study–Act cycles) to adapt interventions to local school contexts. Chapter 6 considers the potential value of combining improvement science and online learning. Chapter 7 concludes the volume with a set of reflections on the major benefits and implications of integrating improvement science more firmly in evaluation.

Collectively, the case chapters in this volume offer an inspiring review of state-of-the-art improvement science applications, providing a broad range of analytical strategies, data visualization techniques, and data collection strategies to be potentially applied in future evaluation contexts. Whereas the cases do not elucidate explicit connections to evaluation, several themes cutting across the cases speak directly to core themes in evaluation. These themes include a persistent focus on systems thinking, a determination to capture and better understand variation and contextual complexity, as well as a sustained commitment to generative learning about projects and programs: all issues of great concern to evaluators. The final chapter connects these themes, among others, with current trends in evaluation.

It is our hope that the volume will promote cross-talk between evaluation and improvement science—a field that continues to gain traction in an increasing range of public policy areas. From this perspective, the issue comes at just the right time to help both producers and users of evaluations to see the potential benefits of a closer engagement with improvement science.

References

Cousins, J. B., & Leithwood, K. A. (1986). Current empirical research on evaluation utilization. *Review of Educational Research, 56*, 331–364.

Cousins, J. B., & Shulha, L. M. (2006). A comparative analysis of evaluation utilization and its cognate fields of inquiry: Current issues and trends. In I. Shaw, J. Greene, & M. Mark (Eds.), *Handbook of evaluation: Program, policy, and practice* (pp. 266–291). Thousand Oaks, CA: Sage.

Hofstetter, C. H., & Alkin, M. (2003). Evaluation use revisited. In T. Kellaghan, D. L. Stufflebeam, & L. Wingate (Eds.), *International handbook of educational evaluation* (pp. 189–196). Boston, MA: Kluwer.

Kenney, C. C. (2008). *The best practice: How the new quality movement is transforming medicine.* New York, NY: Public Affairs.

Leviton, L. C., & Hughes, E. F. X. (1981). Research on the utilization of evaluations: A review and synthesis. *Evaluation Review, 5,* 525–549.

Moen, R. D., Nolan, T. W., & Provost, L. P. (2012). *Quality improvement through planned experimentation.* New York, NY: McGraw-Hill.

Rother, M. (2009). *Toyota kata: Managing people for improvement, adaptiveness and superior results.* New York, NY: McGraw-Hill Professional.

Weiss, C. H. (1998). *Evaluation* (2nd ed.). Upper Saddle River, NJ: Prentice-Hall.

Christina A. Christie
Moira Inkelas
Sebastian Lemire
Editors

CHRISTINA A. CHRISTIE *is professor and chair of the Department of Education in the Graduate School of Education and Information Studies, University of California, Los Angeles.*

MOIRA INKELAS *is an associate professor in the Department of Health Policy and Management in the UCLA Fielding School of Public Health and assistant director of the Center for Healthier Children, Families and Communities.*

SEBASTIAN LEMIRE *is a doctoral candidate in the Social Research Methodology Division in the Graduate School of Education and Information Studies, University of California, Los Angeles.*

NEW DIRECTIONS FOR EVALUATION • DOI: 10.1002/ev

Christie, C. A., Lemire, S., & Inkelas, M. (2017). Understanding the similarities and dis-
tinctions between improvement science and evaluation. In C. A. Christie, M. Inkelas &
S. Lemire (Eds.), *Improvement Science in Evaluation: Methods and Uses. New Directions for
Evaluation, 153,* 11–21.

1

Understanding the Similarities and Distinctions Between Improvement Science and Evaluation

Christina A. Christie, Sebastian Lemire, Moira Inkelas

Abstract

*In this chapter, we discuss the similarities and points of departure between im-
provement science and evaluation, according to use, valuing, and methods—
three dimensions of evaluation theory to which all theorists attend (Christie
& Alkin, 2012). Using these three dimensions as a framework for discussion,
we show some of the ways in which improvement science and evaluation are
similar and how they are different in terms of purposes, goals, and processes.
By doing so we frame the illustrative cases of improvement science that follow
in this issue.* © 2017 Wiley Periodicals, Inc., and the American Evaluation
Association.

Improvement science is an approach to increasing knowledge that leads
to an improvement of a product, process, or system (Moen, Nolan, &
Provost, 2012). Evaluation is a systematic process designed to yield
information about the merit, worth, or value of "something" and, for the
context of this journal issue, that something is assumed to be a program
or policy. These two approaches have much in common, but little has been
written about the ways in which they are similar, different, or how they
can be used cooperatively. In what follows, we consider similarities and
distinctions across three dimensions of evaluation theory: use, valuing, and

methods. Before advancing this comparison, however, an important distinction about the theoretical foundations of improvement science and evaluation is called for.

Theoretical Foundations of Evaluation and Improvement Science

Evaluation has a theoretical literature that is composed of an array of models for how best to practice evaluation. Simply consider the prescriptive models for theory-based and realist evaluation, utilization-focused and empowerment evaluation, and, perhaps more recently, the surge of interest in developmental evaluation. These theories have an ultimate goal, which articulates what is assumed to be the primary purpose of evaluation from the perspective of that theoretical approach. Common for all of these evaluation theories is their prescription of distinctive elements that help to delimit the approach and distinguish it from other approaches. For example, there are theoretical approaches that define evaluation as the science of valuing (Scriven, 2003) whereas others see the ultimate goal to be program improvement (Patton, 2008) or empowerment (Fetterman, 1994).

For a theory to be translated or applied in practice, it must be delineated in terms of the processes and procedures that lead to the actualization of the theory's goal. Not all prescriptions for practice are theories, however. A theory must have an identifiable "character"—specific goals and purposes that are articulated and complemented by a set of procedures for achieving these. Not all procedures or methods are unique to a particular theoretical approach. And although these approaches have different goals for evaluation, they do share common procedures, such as, for example, the use of qualitative data collection strategies. Unfortunately, and as observed by Miller and Campbell (2006), some of these evaluation theories prescribe what evaluators should do but rarely how to do it.

Improvement science differs from evaluation in this regard. Improvement science emerged from the study of production in the early 20th century, Deming's profound knowledge, emphasizing systems theory, analytical studies, the study of variation, and human psychology in production systems (Langley et al., 2009). Although differences about the precise definition of improvement science exist, there is general agreement on the ultimate purpose of improvement science, that being continuous improvement through systematic study. Improvement is accomplished through design or redesign of products and/or processes and improvement of the system that produces the products and processes (Moen et al., 2012). Painting in broad strokes, this unifying goal is arguably more focused than the many different goals prescribed by evaluation theory. And, perhaps as a result, improvement science is typically more operational, offering not just a unifying goal but also, and perhaps more important, guidance on how to achieve that goal.

There are, of course, different models for how to do improvement science, different procedures for practice. These models, however, are not grounded or motivated by epistemological or ideological positions. Rather, they are defined by a different set of procedures and techniques that are informed by a shared postpositivist epistemology. In general, it is this pragmatic approach to knowledge production that results in a broad array of concrete techniques and tools to be potentially applied in evaluative contexts. Before illustrating the applications of improvement science, we situate improvement science in the context of use, valuing, and methods dimensions of evaluation.

The Use Dimensions of Evaluation and Improvement Science

Use refers to the extent to which the practices and procedures of the evaluation are designed to promote the goal of using an evaluation's process or findings (Weiss, 1998). Use is also a dimension of practice where evaluation and improvement science share common ground. Whereas use is a central aim of evaluation, as evidenced by the rich literature on this topic, it has always been defined in relation to (and as a possible outcome of) different evaluation activities. Use defined as improvement is what defines improvement science. The development of improvement science techniques, methods, and concepts emerges from the idea of process, product, or systems change. Improvement is the driver of improvement science.

There are several key ideas and processes that are associated with evaluation models that have as the primary goal producing actionable evidence for improvement of programs and decision making that are shared with improvement processes. This is not surprising given that the goal of improvement science is to generate information that leads to testing a change. Thus, the primary goals and outcomes of use theories are well aligned with the goals of improvement science, as are many of the procedures associated with use approaches, such as stakeholder engagement and participation.

Improvement science is often highly collaborative with a specific role for people closest to the process, similar to participatory evaluation approaches that have grown out of evaluation use approaches, such as practical participatory evaluation (Cousins & Earl, 1992). Key here is that both provide a process for connecting practitioners to an evaluative process through engagement. Buy-in is a necessary condition in such participatory processes, which often serves to reduce fears and anxiety that are related to the conduct of evaluative processes (Donaldson, Gooler, & Scriven, 2002) and thus increases the likelihood that learning will occur as a result of the process. Accordingly, intimate knowledge of processes that are the target of improvement is fundamental to improvement science. In fact, in improvement science leaving the process owners out of the change process is looked down upon and associated with failure to improve (Kaplan, Provost, Froehle, & Margolis, 2012).

Another necessary condition for success in a participatory evaluation process is the capacity of stakeholders to think "evaluatively" (Vo, 2013). Evaluative thinking is a type of critical thinking that is specific to evaluation, where systematic evidence is used to construct arguments and value judgments that are contextually relevant (Vo, 2013). Although this particular type of cognitive process is not discussed in relationship to improvement science, it is easy to see how evaluative thinking is also necessary for good improvement processes to occur.

In contrast, improvement science emphasizes systems thinking and knowledge of the psychological processes that generate change (Deming, 2000). Whereas interest in systems thinking is growing among evaluators, it has yet to become a backbone of our practice. The concepts, tools, and techniques of systems thinking are arguably still far—both in conceptual and operational terms—from most evaluation practice. As such, it is probably more talked about than practiced. Similarly, and perhaps somewhat more surprising, the attention to the psychological processes of change have been less salient in evaluation. This is surprising given the intellectual roots of evaluation in social psychology. Yet, and in spite of the obvious relevance, the role of and attention awarded behavioral change theories, as just one example, are limited in evaluation, both in theory and practice. Central to the improvement scientists' practice is the knowledge of psychology of change. The explicit use of psychology as well as the learning method itself (i.e., adaptation of the scientific method for action-oriented learning) is core to improvement science as a change management method. The resultant array of change concepts speaks to this point and should be of wide interest to evaluators.

Improvement science also differs from evaluation use approaches in that improvement does not focus on social accountability. Rather, because the focus is local, emphasizing the implementation of small, rapid cycle tests of changes, data are often collected for use by service delivery providers (i.e., a physician), so that outcomes can be improved. Improvement science is intended to be practiced by "process owners" (people in systems), why the focus is usually quite concrete (leading to specific action), as opposed to being broad (i.e., we need a culture change).

While presenting on improvement science at a meeting of the American Evaluation Association, we fielded questions about how improvement science and developmental evaluation may or may not be similar, and we hope to clarify this for our readers. Michael Patton, a well-known evaluation use researcher and theorist, has recently written on and popularized an evaluation approach referred to as developmental evaluation (2010). Developmental evaluation "tracks and attempts to make sense of what emerges under conditions of complexity, documenting and interpreting the dynamics, interactions, and interdependencies that occur as innovations unfold" (Patton, 2010, p. 7). Formative evaluation focuses on improvements, like improvement science, rather than on developments, which is the focus of developmental evaluation. In the first chapter of his book, Patton describes how in developmental evaluation, the evaluator brings evaluative thinking and data to the development of program approaches for different groups of recipients and policies. Accepting this definition, although improvement science and developmental evaluation share the focus on quick data collection cycles that take into account the system dynamics, Patton would argue that these processes are different in their purpose and goal. Moreover, developmental evaluation does not begin with the defined theory, rather outcomes emerge through the evaluative process. Improvement science, however, usually begins with identifying clear, specific, and measurable outcomes, exactly what Patton describes should not take place in a developmental evaluation.

The Valuing Dimensions of Evaluation and Improvement Science

Valuing describes approaches that emphasize the importance of how, by whom, and in what way value judgments about programs are determined in evaluation. Many evaluators view their work in terms of the ways in which it may contribute to social good. Paraphrasing from Ernest House (1980), evaluation determines who gets what. As such, social justice oriented evaluators, such as Ernest House (1980), Jennifer Greene (2016), and Donna Mertens (1999), argue that the evaluator should take a position on evaluation as a process for improving social conditions and disrupting systematic power imbalances. In this way, evaluation deliberately addresses the social, economic, and political systems in which programs and policies are developed and implemented, sometimes with the aim of challenging the status quo.

In improvement science, the good that comes of the process is the improvement in quality, which should lead to better outcomes and services for program beneficiaries. This point, however, is not taken up ideologically. Instead, quality improvement focuses on stakeholders identifying the needed areas of improvement in a system, toward identifying and testing relevant solution(s). This kind of systems thinking is aligned with the work of Meadows (2008) where a system is an "interconnected set of elements that is coherently organized in a way that achieves something" (p. 11). From this perspective, improvement science does not by definition focus on systems issues in an effort to improve the social, economic, or political system conditions (though these conditions may be influenced).

Related to social justice, evaluation scholars in recent years have focused on the role of culture in evaluation and the various ways in which culture, race, and class shape the evaluation process. Theoretical writings have addressed issues of cultural diversity and why and how evaluators need to reflect on and engage in thoughtful practices that respect the culture of the evaluation context. Culture refers not only to race, ethnicity, social class,

NEW DIRECTIONS FOR EVALUATION • DOI: 10.1002/ev

language, sexual orientation, age, and gender but also to organizational culture and institutions such as government, education, family, and religion (American Evaluation Association, 2011).

Issues of cultural competence are also addressed in quality improvement and the improvement science literature. When searching the literature, there are improvement science studies that focus on how services can be improved toward better alignment with the values of a particular group, such as HIV-positive men who have sex with men, or African American women with Type II diabetes. The literature does not, however, address issues related to the ways in which culture affects the process of improvement science itself, similar to what has emerged in the evaluation literature. Whereas the evaluation literature addresses the importance of evaluation taking into account the culture of the actors and contexts in which an evaluation takes place (as is also the case with improvement science), a growing body of literature also concerns the ways in which cultural competence in evaluation "is a stance taken toward culture" that "emerges from an ethical commitment to fairness and equity for stakeholders" (American Evaluation Association, 2011).

The sustained interest in valuing among evaluators should be viewed in the broader context of evaluation as a driver for social betterment. In this spirit, and especially in the era of accountability, program performance takes center stage. One unfortunate consequence emerging from this heavy focus on outcomes is the limited room for programs to fail, especially when aiming for large-scale, longer-term changes. Fear of failure pervades evaluation. In contradistinction, learning from error is an important aspect of improvement science. Improvement science is a process of testing change. In the spirit of this goal, failure is expected and accepted. By removing the high stakes associated with studying program impact and instead studying small iterative changes, mistakes are less consequential and change more manageable. A space for error has been carved out.

The Methods Dimensions of Evaluation and Improvement Science

Methods refer to those approaches that have as the primary goal methodological rigor and knowledge generation. Early evaluation practice was grounded in a positivist search for effective solutions to social problems (Shadish, Cook, & Leviton, 1991). From this perspective, stringent application of research methodology (e.g., Campbell's "Experimenting Society") was used to produce evidence of a program's success. Successful programs would then be replicated and transferred to other problems or contexts and those not proven successful would be terminated (Cronbach et al., 1980). These evaluation experiments often proved difficult to sustain and rarely provided contextually valid data (e.g., Cronbach et al., 1980; Patton, 2008; Shadish et al., 1991). And even when positive results were not obtained, programs often continued (Patton, 2008; Shadish et al., 1991). As a result, evaluators have increasingly turned their attention toward outcome patterns and variations across different implementation settings, times, and contexts.

Identifying and understating variation in outcomes is also a very important part of the improvement science methodological toolbox. Part of what explains variation in program outcomes is the complexity of the contexts in which programs are delivered. Deming (2000) argued that a key to solving most quality problems is recognizing that often what we are attempting to change are complex systems. A common mistake is to assume that it is one component of a system, or one variable, that is causing the problem. If this were the case, innovations could always be tested using more traditional evaluation designs such as randomized controlled trials (RCT). But in fields such as health care or education, the effects of single variables are most often dwarfed by the complexity of the system in which they are embedded (Berwick, 2008). So, it is necessary to understand the component processes that make up the system and how they work together in order to understand the roots of the problem and generate innovative solutions. Sometimes quality can be improved by merely tweaking the system, that is, making small changes that enable the system to function in context the way it was designed to function. But other times the system must be redesigned from the ground up or major components changed. This framework consists of the following components: clear shared goals; sensitive measures to chart progress; deep understanding of the problems/barriers that impede success; sources of innovations, grounded in explicit theories of the problem; and mechanisms for comparing/researching innovations and systematically testing whether proposed changes are actually improvements (see Juran & DeFeo, 2010; Langley et al., 2009; Rother, 2009). These five components bring focus to the improvement process and highlight the kind of evaluative process necessary to establish that a hypothesized change is, in fact, an improvement.

Another crucial characteristic of the methodological approach taken by improvement scientists has to do with the intended outcome of their work. Whereas traditional evaluators have focused on demonstrating significant improvements in average outcomes compared with the status quo, the focus in improvement science is equally on reducing variability in outcomes. A true improvement is one that can be counted on to work for most everyone, not just for a few participants and not only with a subset of circumstances. Reducing variability requires that innovations be grounded in explicit theories of change, for it is critical to know not only that an innovation works but also why it works in a particular context. Having theories that explain variability across contexts is also critical for future scaling of an intervention to function in a wide array of contexts.

There are many evaluation models that Christie and Alkin (2012) classify as methods approaches, which focus on understanding how programs work on average with a given sample, in a particular context. Thus, whereas improvement science shares epistemological "land" with methods-focused evaluation approaches, methods approaches such as the RCT and some quasi-experimental approaches do not have improvement as the primary goal; rather, these studies are taken up to study impact, with less attention on understanding variation and more on how the program works on average when implemented with fidelity. In contrast, improvement science places a heavy emphasis on learning from variation and learning about the specific conditions under which processes fail to work.

In evaluation, many of these designs, but in particular the RCT, assume that the program is already performing at its best, and the purpose of the study is to determine whether there is a causal link between the program and its intended outcomes. Improvement science uses many of the practices and procedures used by methods approach evaluation theorists. However, these approaches are used in different ways and for different purposes. For example, randomization (the scientific method) can be part of small-scale tests in improvement to address the question, "What happens when one group of people do this and another group does not? How does the outcome differ?" The distinction is that these RCTs are not full-scale field trials. Rather, randomization is used throughout the small-scale testing and implementation phases of improvement science in an attempt to isolate the change in an outcome if a program process is tweaked or changed in a particular way. Also, although the logic of randomization works the same way in improvement science and evaluation, an important distinction is that improvement scientists do not view randomized experiments as the "gold standard" for producing evidence because context is so essential to improvement; the goal is prediction not estimation so any methods that do not open the black box are suboptimal.

For improvement science, the scientific method is used for action-oriented learning. Thus, use of randomization is an admission of a lack of knowledge about something, and improvement is in pursuit of that knowledge, otherwise the ability to predict the impact of a change under varying conditions is compromised. In evaluation, random assignment is usually applied in the context of large-scale studies and the program beneficiaries are most often the unit at which random assignment is most desired as it is the purpose of these studies to address the question of overall program impact on a given set of outcomes. It is typically a design feature of large-scale studies, as opposed to a useful logic potentially applied in small-scale, iterative learning cycles.

Another key feature of improvement science that is shared with methods focused evaluation approaches is the use of program theories, both theories of change and theories of action. Theories about program processes and their connection to program outcomes are critical in improvement science as they frame the ideas for change in relationship between the aims of the improvement process. These theories are often depicted in driver diagrams. Driver diagrams articulate measurable changes in outcomes, how the processes that are involved in the change process will advance measurable outcomes. They are very similar to logic models as they often incorporate elements of both the theory of change and theory of action. The processes articulated in the driver diagram are ideally evidence based. Like theories of change and action on evaluation, they also often incorporate the expert knowledge of those working within the context or system.

The theories in improvement science are then used to guide small tests of the changes in processes and procedures over a short period of time that will result in improvement. In improvement science, the scale of the test comes from degree of belief (confidence that the idea will lead to the desired outcome, readiness of the system for the change, cost of failure). This is also where the use of an RCT might come in. Randomization and replication are used in improvement science at the smallest scale and during implementation, whereby procedures are revised and refined based on the data generated from the improvement process, and the theory is revised along the way. This process is collaborative and participatory, with those leading the improvement process (akin to the evaluator) and those implementing the processes (akin to program staff) working together to collect and understand data.

Theories are often tested on a small scale and then brought to scale later in the process. Thus, it is critical that the immediate outcomes in the driver diagrams be well articulated, as they may be the only outcomes in the theory that are tested. In evaluation, we often focus on measuring the longer term outcomes of the theory or its impact. Consequently, theories in improvement science are often more dynamic that those that are developed in the context of an evaluation study that may focus on measuring outcomes 3, 5, or even 10 years after program implementation. Whereas the idea of incremental scale-up is nothing new in evaluation (see Weiss, 2010), the procedures and tools for sequential learning are much more formalized and empirically tested in the context of improvement science.

The Way Forward

Evaluation and improvement science intertwine across the use, valuing, and methods dimensions. Cutting across these three dimensions, the cases presented in this issue illustrate a broad range of improvement science applications, offering analytical strategies, data visualization techniques, and data collection strategies to potentially further and support the use of improvement science as an evaluation strategy in specific contexts.

References

American Evaluation Association. (2011). *Public statement on cultural competence in evaluation*. Fairhaven, MA: Author. Retrieved from http://www.eval.org/p/cm/ld/fid=92

Berwick, D. M. (2008). The science of improvement. *Journal of the American Medical Association, 299*(10), 1182–1184.

Christie, C. A., & Alkin, M. C. (2012). An evaluation theory tree. In M.C. Alkin (Ed.), *Evaluation roots* (2nd ed.). Thousand Oaks, CA: Sage.

Cousins, J. B., & Earl, L. M. (1992). The case for participatory evaluation. *Educational Evaluation and Policy Analysis, 14*(4), 397–418.

Cronbach, L. J., Ambron, S. R., Dornbusch, S. M., Hess, R. D., Hornik, R. C., Phillips, D. C., ... Weiner, S. S. (1980). *Toward reform of program evaluation*. San Francisco, CA: Jossey-Bass.

Deming, W. E. (2000). *Out of the crisis*. Boston, MA: MIT Press.

Donaldson, S. I., Gooler, L. E., & Scriven, M. (2002). Strategies for managing evaluation anxiety: Toward a psychology of program evaluation. *American Journal of Evaluation, 23*(3), 261–273.

Fetterman, D. M. (1994). Steps of empowerment evaluation: From California to Cape Town. *Evaluation and Program Planning, 17*(3), 305–313.

Greene, J. (2016). *Advancing equity: Cultivating an evaluation habit. Evaluation for an equitable society*. Charlotte, NC: Information Age Publishing.

House, E. R. (1980). *Evaluating with validity*. Beverly Hills, CA: Sage.

Juran, J. M., & DeFeo, J. A. (2010). *Juran's quality handbook—the complete guide to performance excellence* (6th ed.). New York, NY: McGraw-Hill.

Kaplan, H. C., Provost, L. P., Froehle, C. M., & Margolis, P. A. (2012). The model for understanding success in quality (MUSIQ): Building a theory of context in healthcare quality improvement. *BMJ Quality and Safety, 21*, 13–20.

Langley, G. J., Moen, R. D., Nolan, K. M., Nolan, T. W., Norman, C. L., & Provost, L. P. (2009). *The improvement guide* (2nd ed.). San Francisco, CA: Jossey-Bass.

Meadows, D. H. (2008). *Thinking in systems*. White River Junction, VT: Chelsea Green Publishing.

Mertens, D. M. (1999). Inclusive evaluation: Implications of a transformative theory for evaluation. *American Journal of Evaluation, 20*(1), 1–14.

Miller, R. L., & Campbell, R. (2006). Taking stock of empowerment evaluation—An empirical review. *American Journal of Evaluation, 27*(3), 296–319.

Moen, R. D., Nolan, T. W., & Provost, L. P. (2012). *Quality improvement through planned experimentation*. New York, NY: McGraw Hill.

Patton, M. Q. (2008). *Utilization-focused evaluation* (4th ed.). Thousand Oaks, CA: Sage.

Patton, M. Q. (2010). *Developmental evaluation. Applying complexity concepts to enhance innovation and use*. New York, NY: Guilford Press.

Rother, M. (2009). *Toyota kata: Managing people for improvement, adaptiveness and superior results*. San Francisco, CA: McGraw-Hill Professional.

Scriven, M. (2003). Evaluation in the new millennium: The transdisciplinary view. In S. I. Donaldson & M. Scriven (Eds.), *Evaluating social programs and problems: Visions for the new millennium* (pp. 19–42). Mahwah, NJ: Erlbaum.

Shadish, W. R., Cook, T. D., & Leviton, L. C. (1991). *Foundations of program evaluation: Theories of practice*. Newbury Park, CA: Sage.

Vo, A. (2013). *Toward a definition of evaluative thinking* (Unpublished dissertation). University of California, Los Angeles.

Weiss, C. H. (1998). *Evaluation* (2nd ed.). Upper Saddle River, NJ: Prentice-Hall.

Weiss, C. H. (2010). Scaling impact. *The Evaluation Exchange, XV*(1). Boston, MA: Author. Retrieved from www.hfrp.org

CHRISTINA A. CHRISTIE *is professor and chair of the Department of Education in the Graduate School of Education and Information Studies, University of California, Los Angeles.*

SEBASTIAN LEMIRE *is a doctoral candidate in the Social Research Methodology Division in the Graduate School of Education and Information Studies, University of California, Los Angeles.*

MOIRA INKELAS *is associate professor in the Department of Health Policy and Management in the Fielding School of Public Health, University of California, Los Angeles, and assistant director of the Center for Healthier Children, Families and Communities.*

NEW DIRECTIONS FOR EVALUATION • DOI: 10.1002/ev

Lemire, S., Christie, C. A., & Inkelas, M. (2017). The methods and tools of improvement science. In C. A. Christie, M. Inkelas & S. Lemire (Eds.), *Improvement Science in Evaluation: Methods and Uses. New Directions for Evaluation, 153*, 23–33.

2

The Methods and Tools of Improvement Science

Sebastian Lemire, Christina A. Christie, Moira Inkelas

Abstract

Rooted in ideas from operations research in the 1930s, improvement science bloomed in the healthcare literature during the 1990s and has since then spread rapidly across fields such as management, social work, behavioral economics, and most recently education (Lewis, 2015). So what is thing called "improvement science"? What is the intellectual foundation of improvement science? And what does it look like in real-world applications? What, if anything, might we, as evaluators, learn from the techniques and tools of improvement science? These are questions that will be addressed in this chapter. © 2017 Wiley Periodicals, Inc., and the American Evaluation Association.

Toward a Definition of Improvement Science

Improvement science means many different things to many different people. Perhaps because of the rapid cross-field fertilization, the term "improvement science" has often been used interchangeably with terms such as "science of improvement," "continuous improvement," "system improvement," and even "scientific quality improvement," to name but a few (Health Foundation, 2011). Despite this rich and diverse terminological landscape, or perhaps as a result thereof, harvesting an explicit definition of improvement science is not an easy task. As noted by Marshall, Provost, and Dixon-Woods (2013), the lack of consensus on a definition may just indicate the preparadigm phase in which improvement science currently resides, despite its growing popularity.

The label "science of improvement" emerges with Langley and colleagues' publication of *The Improvement Guide* in 1996 (Perla, Provost & Parry, 2013). Without offering an explicit definition of the term, Langley et al. (2009) identify William E. Deming's "system of profound knowledge" as the intellectual foundation for improvement science (p. 75). Following Deming, a system of profound knowledge is structured around four types of knowledge:

1. Knowledge of systems
2. Knowledge of psychology
3. Knowledge of variation
4. Knowledge of how knowledge grows

Given the foundational role of these four types of knowledge, brief consideration of what is meant by each is called for. Knowledge of systems refers to an understanding of systems as "an interdependent group of items, people, or processes working together toward a common purpose" (Langley et al., 2009, p. 77). For the improvement scientist, consideration of these interdependencies is central when designing, testing, and implementing changes. As noted by Langley et al. (2009), "considering interdependence will also increase the accuracy of our predictions about the impact of changes throughout the system"—a central aim of improvement science (p. 78).

In tandem with knowledge of systems, knowledge of psychology, understanding the human side of change, speaks to the importance of understanding how and in what way interpersonal and social structures influence system processes and performance when designing and implementing changes. Individuals may react or commit to, integrate or expunge, reject or support changes to a system. As such, deploying methods and tools that support the human aspect of change are more likely to lead to successful and sustained improvement.

Another central knowledge component, especially in relation to the measurement of change, is knowledge of variation. As noted by Langley et al. (2009), knowledge of variation involves a distinction between variations in system performance stemming from designed change (special cause variation) versus variations stemming from naturally occurring change (common cause variation). Separating the two types of variation, as well as determining whether a system is influenced by one or the other (or both), is central to testing change.

Finally, knowledge of how knowledge grows is central to ensure successful improvements. Central to this end is the role of predictions about which changes will result in improvements. As Langley and colleagues (2009) remind us, "The more knowledge one has about how the particular system under consideration functions or could function, the better the prediction and the greater the likelihood the change will result in improvement" (p. 81). Building knowledge then, relies on the ability to compare predictions about changes with empirical results (Langley et al., 2009).

Returning to the topic of how to define improvement science, Deming's system of profound knowledge may still fall short of a satisfying definition. This is in large part because it does not specify what improvement science is or is not. The four types of knowledge are simply too broad in their potential application to serve well in this regard. Moreover, the purposes and functions of improvement science are also left unstated. From this perspective, Deming's system of profound knowledge is perhaps better viewed as the intellectual foundation for improvement science, the pillars on which improvement science is grounded.

Resting on the intellectual foundation from Deming, we may consider the two core features of improvement science provided by Langley and colleagues:

1. The idea that improvement emerges from developing, testing, implementing, and spreading change, and
2. The recognition that subject matter experts play a lead role in defining and informing each of those four steps (cited in Perla et al., 2013).

Stated differently, improvement science is about developing, testing, implementing, and spreading change informed by subject matter experts. The orientation toward change is echoed in the observation that improvement science is "a type of practical problem solving, an evidence-based management style, or the application of a theory-driven science of how to bring about system change" (Margolis, Provost, Schoettker, & Britto, 2009, p. 832). From this perspective, improvement science is situated somewhere between change management and research (Health Foundation, 2011).

Informed by the contributions cited here, a working—or at least workable—definition of improvement science for the purpose of this special issue may be offered. Inspired by Langley et al. (2009), among others, we define improvement science as:

> A data-driven change process that aims to systematically design, test, implement, and scale change toward systemic improvement, as informed and defined by the experience and knowledge of subject matter experts.

Admittedly, this is a working definition of improvement science for the purpose of this special issue—to compare and contrast improvement science with evaluation. As is evident from the proposed definition, several aspects of improvement science resonate with key aspects of traditional definitions of evaluation, including the systematic application of data, the use of data to test and scale up changes, the focus on systemic improvement, and the involvement of stakeholders. In this way, much of what improvement science *is* is evaluation. In this volume, we take up these issues and draw the connections necessary for the evaluation field to consider and use improvement science more widely as a strategy for improving program processes and outcomes.

The Model for Improvement—An Operational Framework for Practice

Another fruitful way of understanding improvement science is to examine the principles and operational framework that structure and support the practical application of improvement science. Painting in broad strokes, and expanding on the conceptual grounding laid out in the preceding section, Perla, Provost, and Parry (2013) identify seven propositions that provide the methodological foundation for the science of improvement:

1. The science of improvement is grounded in testing and learning cycles—an approach that in its practical application is structured around repeated Plan–Do–Study–Act (PDSA) cycles (see the subsequent section on the Improvement Science Toolbox).
2. The philosophical foundation of the science of improvement is conceptualistic pragmatism—an understanding of the importance of combining existing subject matter and theory to make predictions about changes to be implemented and tested.
3. The science of improvement embraces a combination of psychology and logic (i.e., a weak form of "psychologism")—an acknowledgment that psychology paired with analytical philosophy, logic, and mathematics provides the grounding for a stronger understanding of multiple dimensions of change.
4. The science of improvement considers the contexts of justification *and* discovery—an understanding that improvement emerges from the interplay between inductive and deductive logic, procedures of discovery and justification (see subsection on logic of PDSA cycles).
5. The science of improvement requires the use of operational definitions—a belief in the importance of conceptual clarity and shared understanding of what improvement is.
6. The science of improvement employs Shewhart's theory of cause systems—a focus on distinguishing between stable and unstable systems, special and common cause variation.
7. Systems theory directly informs the science of improvement—an appreciation that all change takes place in the context of a dynamic and adaptive system, why understanding the system's composition is a fundamental condition for improvement.

Figure 2.1. The Plan–Do–Study–Act Cycle

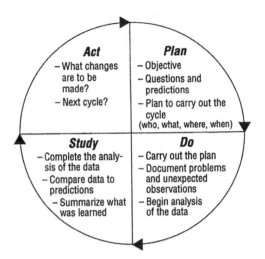

Source: Adapted from Moen, Nolan, & Provost, 2012

The strong association these principles have with the social sciences more generally and evaluation more specifically is considered by Christie, Lemire, and Inkelas (Chapter 1). Collectively, the principles serve to inform the nature of improvement science and in effect to guide improvement science practitioners and theorists (Perla et al., 2013).

In its real-world application, improvement science is framed by the Model for Improvement and structured around PDSA cycles. The Model for Improvement specifies three framing questions for improvement projects:

1. What are we trying to accomplish?
2. How will we know that a change is an improvement?
3. What change can we make that will result in improvement?

The primary function of these questions is to develop changes that will lead to sustained improvement within a system. As Langley et al. (2009) remind us, "Not all changes lead to improvement, but all improvement requires change"—central to improvement science then is to recognize and bridge the difference between the two (p. 357). Toward this aim, the Model for Improvement is realized through the Plan–Do–Study–Act cycle, a re-iterative trial-and-learning process that connects empirical learning with redesign (Langley et al., 2009; Morris & Hiebert, 2011). A generic PDSA cycle is provided in Figure 2.1.

The first step in the cycle is to clearly state the objective of the PDSA cycle as well as the corresponding questions to be answered. Toward this

NEW DIRECTIONS FOR EVALUATION • DOI: 10.1002/ev

aim, the first step also involves the development of an operational plan that details where, when, and by whom the cycle will be implemented. A key component of the plan is a specification of the data collection to be carried out.

Step two in the PDSA cycle revolves around the implementation of the plan. To ensure a systematic and transparent process, documentation of challenges or issues emerging as part of the implementation of the PDSA cycle should be documented. These include any issues related to the data collection.

In the third step of the cycle, attention is awarded the results of the data collection. More specifically, observed patterns in the data are compared with the predicted patterns to identify similarities and contradictions. The aim is to determine whether the data support or undermine the predictions made based on past knowledge and experience.

Informed by this new knowledge, step four provides the opportunity to make additional changes or modifications to the designed change, before (re)running the PDSA cycle. The modifications to be made should be grounded on whether or not the previous steps promoted improvements (however, these are defined under step one). By doing so, a "learning loop" is created, in which iterative rounds of developing, testing, and implementing changes can take place (Langley et al., 2009).

The PDSA cycle can be implemented in many different ways, depending on the specific purpose, context, and conditions of the project. Perhaps needless to say, there is no single right way to carry out PDSA cycles. That being said, Langley et al. (2009, p. 145) highlight three principles for the rigorous "testing of change":

Principle 1:   Test on a small scale and build knowledge sequentially
Principle 2:   Collect data over time
Principle 3:   Include a wide range of conditions in the sequence of tests

Structuring improvement science projects around sequential PDSA cycles is compelling for several reasons. For one thing, the cycle involves a both inductive and deductive reasoning. The interplay is illustrated in Figure 2.2. A deductive approach is deployed when articulating predictions (the "Plan" step) and departures from these are observed (the "Do" step) as part of the PDSA cycle. Subsequently, inductive learning emerges in the "Study" and "Act" steps when divergences between the predictions and the observed outcomes are translated into a set of revised predictions.

Second, the sequential use of PDSA allows for a trail of evidence; advancing a string of small, mutually informed experiments. These trails of evidence may sometimes even develop from small to increasingly larger changes and more formal tests. In this way, the underlying logic of sequential testing aligns closely with Campbell and Stanley's framework for designs (as preexperimental, experimental, or quasiexperimental) and can be traced

Figure 2.2. The Interplay of Inductive and Deductive Logic

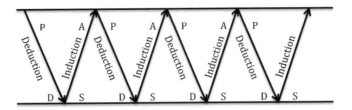

Source: Adapted from Langley et al., 2009

Figure 2.3. Sequential PDSA Cycle

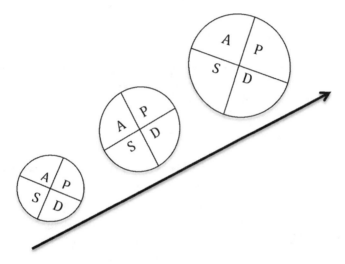

Source: Adapted from Moen, Nolan, & Provost, 2012

even further back to the fundamental principles of the scientific method as articulated by Aristotle and Copernicus, among others (Perla et al., 2013). A generic illustration of sequential experimentation using the PDSA cycle is provided in Figure 2.3.

Third, the progression from smaller to increasingly larger changes also serves to dampen the fear of failure. This is because the piecemeal introduction of small changes constricts the potential adverse consequences of harmful changes. After all, only changes that have proven successful during small-scale testing are further developed and scaled up for the purpose of affecting the system as a whole.

Fourth and finally, and as noted by Langley et al., "Satisfactory prediction of the results of tests conducted over a wide range of conditions is the means to increase the degree of belief that the change will result in improvement" (2009, p. 141). The credibility of the tests can be enhanced by manipulation (e.g., by removing or alternating the change), factorial design strategies, theory (e.g., grounding the change in theory of change), and replication across diverse settings. Again, the sequential nature of the PDSA cycles lends itself well to this incremental testing and confidence building.

Leaving all these compelling features aside, the PDSA cycle is not without its shortcomings. One criticism raised by Langley et al. (2009) is that the small-scale cycles tend to fail to produce impact at the systemic level, which after all, is what improvement science aims for. As noted by Langley et al. (2009), the "small-scale" refers to the testing and not necessarily to the change introduced; the latter may represent a significant departure from practice as usual (p. 102). Another approach to lessen the concern is to coordinate multiple PDSA cycles that collectively promote changes at the system level.

Another issue relates to the varied use and real-world application of PDSA cycles, is that of different degrees of compliance with guidelines for good PDSA practice and reporting, resulting in a lack of transparency about the iterative cycles of improvement, among other things (Taylor et al., 2014). As Taylor and colleagues point out, studies that use PDSA as a "black box" intervention should be cautioned against.

The Control Chart—A Central Tool in the Improvement Science Toolbox

A third way of understanding improvement science is by considering the core tools that support and characterize improvement science. A plethora of tools and methods have been developed to support different stages of the improvement science (and even specific steps of the PDSA cycle). These include tools for developing a change, testing a change, implementing a change, and spreading a change. Many of these are illustrated in the case chapters comprising this volume. Interested readers are also encouraged to find inspiration in the comprehensive list of improvement science tools provided in the appendix of the improvement guide (Langley et al., 2009). However, given the purpose and page limits of the present volume, this is not the place to consider all of these. Instead, consideration is given to the use of control charts—a useful (yet relatively rare tool) in the context of evaluation.

Control Charts—What Are They?

Control charts, also referred to as process behavior charts or Shewhart charts, comprise a central statistical tool in improvement science. Developed by Walter Shewhart in the context of improving production lines, control charts graphically depict outcome patterns over time. Control charts typically consist of a centerline (e.g., a mean or media) and a set of corresponding control limits (e.g., ±2 standard deviations of the centerline).

At root, control charts are about analyzing process variation over time. As noted by Moen, Nolan, and Provost (2012, p. 286), control charts offer a formal approach for distinguishing between:

- *Common cause variation (noise).* This is variation stemming from causes that are inherent in the system (process or product) over time, affect everyone working in the system, and affect all outcomes of the system.
- *Special cause variation.* This is variation rooted in causes that are not part of the system (process or product) all the time or do not affect everyone, but arise because of specific circumstances.

The upper and lower control limits in control charts reflect the boundary between these two types of variation. Outcome patterns within the boundaries are considered expected, natural variation in the system, whereas outcome variations outside of these boundaries are considered signals of special cause variation, often subject to further analysis. In the context of improvement science, this demarcation is of central importance because it allows for the identification of improvements stemming from system changes. In this way, the upper and lower control limits in control charts are pivotal in distinguishing between random variation (i.e., noise) and special cause variation, reflecting "true" signals of change.

For the purpose of establishing upper and lower control limits in control charts, a baker's dozen of guidelines has been suggested, including:

- ±3 sigma from the centerline
- ±2 standard deviations of the centerline
- ±3 standard deviations of the centerline

These guidelines are arbitrary in the sense that their application tends to be based on equal parts convention and subjective preference. As just one example, and as noted by Murray and Provost (2011), the three-sigma guideline is grounded on "experience" rather than statistical theory (p. 160). The statistically oriented reader will probably recognize the other two guidelines' reliance on statistical theory. In real-world practice, the use of ±3 standard deviations of the centerline appears to be the most prevalent among improvement science practitioners, at least within the context of improvement science projects in the health sciences.

An illustrative example of a control chart is provided in Figure 2.4. The dataset supporting the estimation of the control charts stems from the Magnolia Community Project—an improvement science project in the social welfare sector. The outcome variable of interest is a coverage score, representing the degree of care-related concerns covered during meetings between service providers and clients. The coverage score ranges from 0

Figure 2.4. Control Chart for Coverage Scores (by Month)

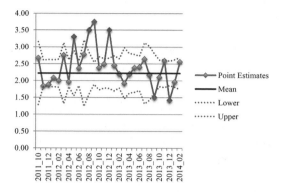

to 4 (with 4 representing complete coverage) for each of these meetings. A total of 850 individual meetings were scored in the period from October 2011 to February 2014.

As Figure 2.4 shows, several point estimates indicate special cause variation: four point estimates indicate variation above the expected common cause variation and two point estimates indicate variation lower than expected common cause variation. In the context of improvement science, these point estimates would motivate further analyses to identify the special cause(s) that produced the observed pattern. For example, the two figures might prompt an analysis of any systematic changes that were made to the organization in the summer of 2012, aiming to identify the cause that generated the pattern in the data. This would involve allocation of human resources and time and potentially lead to conclusions and decisions on future systematic changes to be made in the organization.

In summary, improvement science cannot be defined by any one process or procedure. For the purpose of this volume, we define improvement science as a data-driven change process that aims to systematically design, test, implement, and scale change toward systemic improvement, as informed and defined by the experience and knowledge of subject matter experts. In its practical application, improvement science is framed by the Model for Improvement and structured around PDSA cycles. A central tool for identifying special cause variation is the control chart.

References

Health Foundation. (2011). *Report: Improvement science*. Retrieved from http://www. health.org.uk/publication/improvement-science

Langley, G. J., Moen, R. D., Nolan, K. M., Nolan, T. W., Norman, C. L., & Provost, L. P. (2009). *The improvement guide* (2nd ed.). San Francisco, CA: Jossey-Bass.

Lewis, C. (2015). What is improvement science? Do we need it in education? *Educational Researcher, 44*(1), 54–61.

Margolis, P., Provost, L. P., Schoettker, P. J., & Britto, M. T. (2009). Quality improvement, clinical research, and quality improvement research—Opportunities for integration. *Pediatric Clinics of North America, 56*, 831–841.

Marshall, M., Provost, L. P., & Dixon-Woods, M. (2013). Promotion of improvement as a science. *Lancet, 381*, 419–421.

Moen, R. D., Nolan, T. W., & Provost, L. P. (2012). *Quality improvement through planned experimentation.* New York, NY: McGraw Hill.

Morris, A. K., & Hiebert, J. (2011). Creating shared instructional products: An alternative approach to improving teaching. *Educational Researcher, 40*, 5–14.

Murray, S. K., & Provost, L. P. (2011). *The health care data guide: Learning from data for improvement.* San Francisco, CA: Jossey-Bass.

Perla, R. J., Provost, L. P., & Parry, G. J. (2013). Seven propositions of the science of improvement: Exploring foundations. *Quality Management in Health Care, 22*(3), 170–186.

Taylor, M. J., McNicholas, C., Nicolay, C., Darzi, A., Bell, D., & Reed, J. E. (2014). Systematic review of the application of the plan-do-study-act method to improve quality in healthcare. *BMJ Quality and Safety, 23*, 290–298.

SEBASTIAN LEMIRE is a doctoral candidate in the Social Research Methodology Division in the Graduate School of Education and Information Studies, University of California, Los Angeles.

CHRISTINA A. CHRISTIE is professor and chair of the Department of Education in the Graduate School of Education and Information Studies, University of California, Los Angeles.

MOIRA INKELAS is associate professor in the Department of Health Policy and Management in the Fielding School of Public Health, University of California, Los Angeles, and assistant director of the Center for Healthier Children, Families and Communities.

NEW DIRECTIONS FOR EVALUATION • DOI: 10.1002/ev

Brown, C. M., Kahn, R. S., & Goyal, N. K. (2017). Timely and appropriate healthcare access for newborns: A neighborhood-based, improvement science approach. In C. A. Christie, M. Inkelas & S. Lemire (Eds.), *Improvement Science in Evaluation: Methods and Uses. New Directions for Evaluation, 153*, 35–50.

3

Timely and Appropriate Healthcare Access for Newborns: A Neighborhood-Based, Improvement Science Approach

Courtney M. Brown, Robert S. Kahn, Neera K. Goyal

Abstract

Newborns in low-income families often experience delays between birth hospital discharge and the first primary care visit. Delays in primary care can result in inadequate support and education for families and may lead to emergency department (ED) visits for nonurgent conditions. Our intervention sought to reduce average age at first primary care visit to ≤ 9 days of life and reduce nonurgent ED visits by 20% among infants < 6 months old from one low-income neighborhood in Cincinnati, Ohio. We applied improvement science to iteratively address the many family- and system-level barriers to primary care. Improvement science is a structured approach to improving outcomes through ongoing data collection and examination of how specific practices affect performance. Advantages of this approach include the ability to detect incremental changes in outcomes and continuously adapt interventions over time. This chapter discusses the successes and challenges of applying improvement science to our goals. © 2017 Wiley Periodicals, Inc., and the American Evaluation Association.

I n health care, improvement science has been used primarily to increase the reliability with which screening, assessment, or treatment protocols have been executed by medical staff. Improvement science has been less frequently applied to solving complex community health problems, for which outcomes depend on the behaviors of both patients and service providers. This chapter describes the application of improvement science methods to improve healthcare access for infants from one low-income neighborhood in Cincinnati, Ohio. The chapter discusses the benefits and challenges of using an improvement science approach in this context.

The Model for Improvement

We applied improvement science to work toward reducing delays in primary care and nonurgent emergency department (ED) visits locally. We had several reasons for using an improvement science approach to achieve our aims. First, there is no existing well-defined package of interventions to apply to the problem, requiring an iterative approach to develop solutions. Second, many family- and system-level factors contribute to the problem so we anticipated needing to introduce multiple changes to our system over time as we learned more from our data and initial testing. Third, multiple sectors are involved in the solution to the problem, and it is difficult to control conditions across all sectors, so designing a single fully developed intervention did not fit our problem.

As our operational framework, we applied the Model for Improvement, a specific improvement science approach that asks three fundamental questions: What are we trying to accomplish? How will we know that a change is an improvement? What changes can we test that will result in improvement? (Langley, Nolan, Norman, Provost, & Nolan, 1996).

What Are We Trying to Accomplish?

We addressed this question by reviewing the relevant literature, assessing the needs and assets of our target neighborhood, involving stakeholders, and establishing specific objectives for improvement that followed from this diagnostic phase.

Literature Review: Healthcare Access for Newborns from Low-Income Families. Timely access to primary care for newborns is important to avoid medical complications (Shakib, Buchi, Smith, Korgenski, & Young, 2015). Despite legislation mandating minimum hospital stays for mothers and their newborns, prior research suggests that early discharge after delivery remains common, even among those with medical and social risk factors (Goyal, Fager, & Lorch, 2011; Tomashek et al., 2006). A substantial percentage of new mothers—more often those who are young, those with low income, those who are uninsured or publicly insured, and those of racial minorities—do not feel ready for discharge (Bernstein et al., 2007). As a result, potentially avoidable complications including jaundice and feeding difficulties are more likely to go undetected or untreated, resulting in the need for costly rehospitalization (Meara,

NEW DIRECTIONS FOR EVALUATION • DOI: 10.1002/ev

Kotagal, Atherton, & Lieu, 2004; Shakib et al., 2015). Therefore, timely newborn primary care follow-up provides a critical opportunity to offer support and education, as well as identify and mitigate new medical and social problems as they emerge.

Unfortunately, newborns in low-income families are at highest risk of experiencing a delay in care between discharge from the birth hospital and the first primary care visit (Lansky et al., 2006; O'Donnell, Trachtman, Islam, & Racine, 2014). Prior research suggests that low-income families' barriers to primary care include inflexible scheduling practices, transportation barriers, and failure to understand timelines for primary care follow-up (Lannon et al., 1995). Concurrently, inadequate access to primary care may also result in high rates of newborn ED visits for nonurgent conditions, such as mild upper respiratory infections or normal newborn skin rash (Brousseau et al., 2007). These visits are costly to the healthcare system, unnecessarily expose vulnerable newborns to infectious diseases in ED waiting rooms, and likely indicate lack of parental empowerment to identify and address nonurgent newborn health conditions.

Literature Review: Neighborhood-Based Disparities in Healthcare Use and Outcomes. Prior research has demonstrated that both delays in primary care and inappropriate ED use are associated with neighborhood poverty level and other socioeconomic indicators. For example, lower rates of pediatric immunization have been shown for low-income neighborhoods compared with higher income neighborhoods (Chi, Momany, & Jones, 2013; Van Berckelaer, Mitra, & Pati, 2011). Similarly, studies have found relationships between neighborhood poverty and ED use for nonurgent conditions such as otitis media, upper respiratory infections, and gastroenteritis (Suruda, Burns, Knight, & Dean, 2005; Zlotnick, 2007). There is evidence to suggest that interdisciplinary, neighborhood-based approaches may be effective in improving pediatric health outcomes (Nicholas et al., 2005; Spielman et al., 2006). A prominent example is the Harlem Children's Zone Asthma Initiative, which focused on children living in a 60-block geographic area (Spielman et al., 2006). This initiative engaged community health workers to identify environmental asthma triggers during home visits. The community health workers partnered with physicians, nurses, and social workers to implement medical and environmental interventions, resulting in significant decreases in asthma-related school absences, ED visits, and hospitalizations.

Assessing the Needs and Assets of Our Target Neighborhood. Cincinnati, Ohio has among the highest childhood poverty rates in the United States, with 48% of children living below the poverty line (National Center for Children in Poverty, 2011). We focused our intervention in Avondale, one of Cincinnati's poorest neighborhoods. Avondale families are 81% African American and have a median household income of $20,925 per year (2011–2015 American Community Survey 5-Year Estimates). The child poverty rate is 55%, and the preterm birth rate is 14.2% (local unpublished data). Prior to our interventions, only about half of infants from Avondale attended their first newborn primary care visit by 9 days of life. Per 100 Avondale infants under 6 months of age, there were six nonurgent visits to the ED each month. Avondale has a well-developed community infrastructure for social support. Organizations serving Avondale include Avondale Community Development Corporation, Every Child Succeeds home visiting program, several community health worker programs, faith-based organizations, and a local office of the Special Supplemental Nutrition Program for Women Infants and Children (WIC). Cincinnati Children's Hospital Medical Center (CCHMC) is located in Avondale and operates three primary care centers in the Greater Cincinnati area: Pediatric Primary Care (PPC) in Avondale, Hopple Street Primary Care about three miles from Avondale, and Fairfield Primary Care in a suburb of Cincinnati.

Cincinnati is a uniquely well-resourced setting for improvement science. For many years, CCHMC has been a leader in promoting evidence-based care and improving patient outcomes through improvement science approaches in both inpatient and ambulatory care settings. Such initiatives have resulted in sustained reductions in outcomes such as hospital-acquired infections and serious safety events (Bigham et al., 2009; Muething et al., 2012). In-depth, hands-on improvement science training is available to CCHMC project leaders, staff, and trainees to promote a culture within the organization focused on patient safety and systems improvement. In addition to localized learning and implementation, CCHMC's improvement science leaders have also led learning collaboratives with other healthcare institutions to generate new knowledge and new practice for spread to other settings (Anderson et al., 2014; Forrest, Margolis, Seid, & Colletti, 2014).

Since 2010, CCHMC has also embarked on a unique initiative focused on population health that extends beyond the traditional healthcare setting. Specific improvement science projects have focused on reducing infant mortality, injury, obesity, and asthma morbidity in nearby communities. Through this population health initiative, CCHMC has introduced improvement science to other local organizations, fire departments, and schools. Executives from Procter and Gamble and designers from University of Cincinnati's College of Design, Art, Architecture, and Planning have also worked closely with CCHMC, bringing knowledge from other industries to address health system problems. For example, designers have helped create, test, and adapt decision aids to engage patients in health discussions, using the same strategies that product developers use to optimize products with input from end users (Brinkman et al., 2013). In this way, CCHMC has a history of using improvement science to generate new knowledge and new practice for spread to other settings, in addition to improving processes through localized learning.

Involving Stakeholders. A small workgroup was first developed at CCHMC's pediatric primary care center. This workgroup included three pediatricians, a newborn care coordinator (a nurse who was responsible for facilitating newborn visits and coordinating communication between birth hospitals and primary care), a nurse clinical manager, and a project manager. The pediatricians and the nurse clinical manager each had prior training in improvement science methods through at least one of CCHMC's formal improvement science courses. The newborn coordinator had not had formal training but had been exposed to improvement science methods through several prior improvement science initiatives within the primary care center. The project manager had background in managing improvement science projects and was employed by CCHMC's James M. Anderson Center for Health Systems Excellence. The Anderson Center promotes, facilitates, and supports action-oriented health services research and improvement science across CCHMC.

This workgroup drove the project forward and involved other stakeholders as opportunities arose. For example, two additional PPC pediatricians were recruited to be the "place-based physicians" for infants from Avondale. The group engaged frontline staff from a home visitation program to spread messages about the importance of timely primary care and how to manage minor illnesses at home or in primary care. The head of the local WIC program office worked with the group to promote breastfeeding among local mothers. These community partners did not have formal improvement science training but some had prior exposure to the Model for Improvement from involvement in past initiatives. The group also worked with obstetricians and neonatal hospitalists at birth hospitals serving the Avondale neighborhood, some of whom also had formal improvement science training.

Defining Specific Objectives. Improvement science is guided by S.M.A.R.T. aims, which are statements of **S**pecific, **M**easurable, **A**chievable, **R**elevant, and **T**imely goals. We focused our work in one low-income neighborhood in Cincinnati, Ohio. We set the following two S.M.A.R.T. aims:

1. Increase the percentage of newborns who attend their first primary care visit at $\leq$ 9 days of age to 80% by June 30, 2016.
2. Reduce nonurgent ED use by 20% among infants $<$ 6 months of age by June 30, 2016.

How Will We Know that a Change Is an Improvement?

After establishing our objectives, our next step was to create a data infrastructure to measure change over time. To know that a change is an improvement, it is important to establish a baseline for each specific goal prior to beginning interventions. Measurement to evaluate the impact of each intervention continues as interventions are tested. In addition, the data infrastructure should allow for continued data collection after the improvement science project is completed, although the frequency of reporting may be

Figure 3.1. Monthly Percentage of Avondale Newborns at CCHMC Clinics Attending First Primary Care Visit by 9 Days of Life

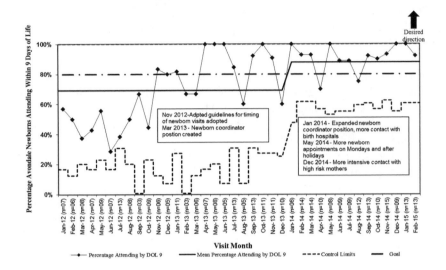

decreased at that stage. This ensures enduring attention to the goal and sustainability of the improvements.

Creating a Data Infrastructure. We created outcome measures for each of our specific aims. In creating our data infrastructure, a balance needed to be achieved between capturing the phenomena we wished to improve, using the data that were available through existing clinical data systems, and measuring outcomes in subsets of the population based on the focus of interventions. Our measures were as follows:

Timeliness of first newborn primary care visit. We used a control chart to track the percentage of newborns who attend their first primary care visit at ≤ 9 days of age (Figure 3.1). We excluded infants born at < 35 weeks gestational age, as we expected they may (appropriately) have later primary care visits due to longer stays in the birth hospital. Because we were interested in this measure on a population level, the denominator would ideally include all newborns born at Avondale. However, initially, data were available only from the electronic health records of infants who had ever scheduled an appointment with a CCHMC primary care center (approximately 65% of Avondale newborns). Similar data were obtained at the University of Cincinnati's pediatric-internal medicine practice, which serves approximately 10% of Avondale newborns. Each primary care practice tracked data on the percentage of their own patient population attending the first primary care visit at ≤ 9 days, with plans to combine these data as new practices serving patients from Avondale joined the initiative.

Figure 3.2. Monthly Rate of Emergency Department Visits for Nonurgent Conditions Among Avondale Infants < 6 Months Old (Per 100 Infants < 6 Months Old in Avondale Population)

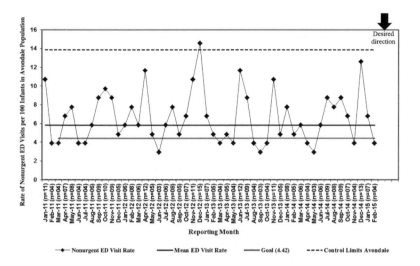

Nonurgent ED visits. We also tracked on a control chart the rate of ED visits for nonurgent conditions among infants from Avondale, defined as number of nonurgent visits per 100 babies in the Avondale population, per census data (Figure 3.2). "Nonurgent" was defined using standard triage levels assigned by ED staff for low acuity. We were interested in this measure on a population level, but data were available only for EDs and urgent care facilities affiliated with CCHMC. Although we believe > 90% of local pediatric ED visits come to CCHMC, any visits to other facilities were not captured. Because interventions were initially implemented on a subset of the population (patients < 60 days of age at CCHMC's primary care centers), we created a separate control chart to track the rate of nonurgent ED visits among that specific population (Figure 3.3).

Evaluation Plan. We used a time series design and statistical process control to evaluate our interventions as we developed them, which allowed for detection of incremental improvements over time. Control charts and statistical process control were used to evaluate the impact of our interventions. As opposed to a traditional pre/postanalysis, in which researchers test a single intervention that they often believe has a high likelihood of success, statistical process control allows for detection of incremental changes over time, which is more appropriate for iteratively designed, multifaceted interventions in which any one individual change has a lower impact on the overall outcome. To discern statistically significant changes over time from normal variation in the data, control charts apply upper and lower control limits at three times the standard deviation below and above the

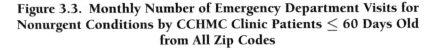

Figure 3.3. Monthly Number of Emergency Department Visits for Nonurgent Conditions by CCHMC Clinic Patients ≤ 60 Days Old from All Zip Codes

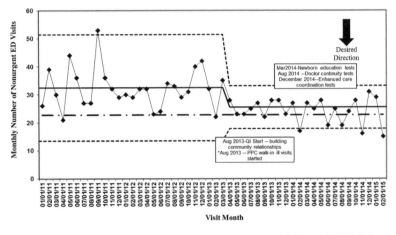

data mean. These control limits account for variation in population sample size at each data point. Observed changes in the data ("shifts") are considered significant when particular patterns are observed in the data, based on the probability that these patterns would occur by chance. When these patterns are observed, the mean is recalculated and adjusted on the control chart. Investigators typically decide a priori how much certainty they want that the observed pattern is not due to chance. Given wide variation in baseline data for our measures, we applied stringent definitions for shifts. We determined we would adjust our centerline when either of the following criteria were met: 8 or more consecutive points either above or below the mean or at least 14 consecutive points alternating above and below the mean. There is < 1% chance of observing these patterns by chance. In addition, "trends" of at least five consecutively increasing or decreasing data points have been shown to be mathematically unlikely due to chance, with the option to make this rule more or less stringent depending on the situation. We chose six consecutively increasing or decreasing data points as our threshold for a trend (Provost & Murray, 2011).

What Changes Can We Test that Will Result in Improvement?

Our workgroup developed a theory of change that we believed would drive improvement in our measures. We then used data to determine what changes could be tested and conducted "Plan-Do-Study-Act" cycles to rapidly test those changes.

Figure 3.4. Simplified Key Driver Diagram for Reduction of Emergency Department Visits for Nonurgent Conditions Among CCHMC Clinic Patients in the First 6 Months of Life

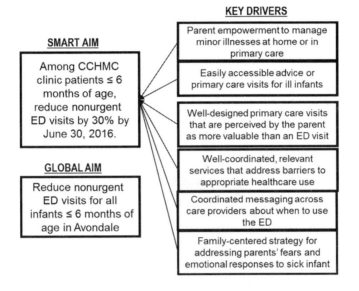

Developing a Theory of Change. The problems we aimed to solve were complex and not likely to change with a single intervention. Because there was no existing package of evidence-based interventions to apply, new knowledge and new practices would need to be generated. The primary workgroup developed a key driver diagram. A key driver diagram is a tool used to organize ideas and visually depict the hypothesized relationships between the aim and the interventions that are tested. The workgroup drew from the literature and clinical experience to identify concepts that they believed to be key drivers of outcomes. (A simplified key driver diagram is shown in Figure 3.4.) The group then listed potential interventions that linked to each key driver. For example, the group believed that parental empowerment to address minor illnesses at home or in primary care would be a key driver in reducing nonurgent ED visits. To have an impact on this driver, the group listed a range of interventions related to developing a portfolio of trusted resources for families to use at home, providing anticipatory guidance about normal infant physiology, and helping families understand who to call for nonurgent health concerns. The wide-ranging list of drivers reflected our theory that reducing ED visits would require a multidisciplinary approach. For example, advice given by home visitors may affect whether parents sought care for their infants in primary care or the ED.

Using Data to Develop Tests of Change. The group used Pareto charts to identify and prioritize ways to target interventions to the patients

Figure 3.5. Pareto Chart of Reasons for Emergency Department Visits for Nonurgent Conditions Among CCHMC Clinic Patients ≤ 60 Days Old from January 2011 to December 2013

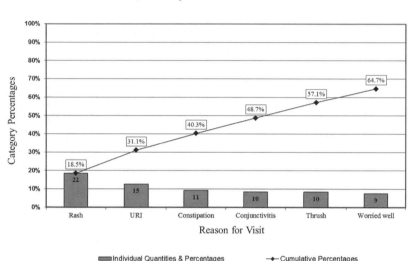

or conditions responsible for the largest numbers of delayed primary care visits or nonurgent ED visits. A Pareto chart is a vertical bar graph in which values are plotted in decreasing order of relative frequency from left to right. Pareto charts are often used to identify the most common reasons for "failure" that can be addressed by specific tests of change. As an example, infants born on or around holidays accounted for a large percentage of the delayed primary care visits. Consequently, the newborn coordinator reserved more appointment slots on the schedule for newborn appointments on days adjacent to holidays (and overbooked newborn appointments when necessary) to ensure that these infants would be seen in a timely manner. Testing this systematic change showed direct impact on timely newborn visits.

Figure 3.5 shows an example of a Pareto chart. Five conditions were found to be responsible for 57% of nonurgent ED visits among infants less than 60 days old. The group tested a series of parent education interventions about these specific conditions. The direct impact of these interventions on nonurgent ED use was difficult to assess, given the many factors influencing the ED visit rate. There was no way to know which infants would develop the conditions and whether these infants would have gone to the ED without the educational interventions. However, we continued to pursue these interventions because of the possibility that they were necessary but insufficient to shift the measure of ED use.

We also learned from qualitative examination of individual cases to develop and adapt our interventions. For example, a mother missed her infant's first primary care appointment because she went to the wrong location. The newborn coordinator communicated closely with this mother and discovered that the mother was socially isolated, spoke English as a second language, and had trouble navigating the healthcare system. We sought ideas for change by working to solve the problem for this single family. The newborn coordinator helped the mother get to the rescheduled primary care appointment by talking her through the directions on her mobile phone and meeting her on the street in front of the clinic. Outside the boundaries of the "regular system," in which the newborn coordinator would hand off any telephone contact to the larger pool of triage nurses after the first completed primary care visit, the newborn coordinator served as a primary point of contact for this mother throughout the first 6 weeks of the infant's life. During this time period, the newborn coordinator received five calls from the mother about minor infant health concerns. The infant had two ill visits in primary care and no ED visits. Although it is impossible to know whether this infant would have had an ED visit otherwise, we considered this close contact with the newborn coordinator a success. After learning all of the steps necessary to help this mother develop a connection to primary care, we identified a potentially scalable strategy to support more mothers who shared characteristics with this one. We tested having the newborn coordinator serve as the primary point of contact through 6 weeks of age for any infant with mothers who indicated that they were socially isolated or that their first language was not English.

Plan–Do–Study–Act (PDSA) Ramps. As outlined in the Model for Improvement, changes were tested through a series of Plan–Do–Study–Act (PDSA) cycles, which provide a systematic method for action-oriented learning. In this approach, a specific change is selected, defined, and planned ("plan"), then implemented ("do"). Once the change is initiated, the team tracks the outcome to determine if improvement has occurred ("study"). Finally, the team "acts" to determine what changes if any need to be made, and the PDSA cycle is repeated. Repeated observations of such tests leading to desired improvements under different conditions, and with increasing scale, supports the decision to adopt the final version of the change permanently. We conducted ramps of PDSA cycles to iteratively develop and improve new processes. As mentioned previously, to empower parents to manage minor illnesses, we developed interventions that included anticipatory guidance and a portfolio of resources for home use. This PDSA ramp evolved over time as shown in Table 3.1. As illustrated by this example, each new test was adapted based on what was learned from the previous test. In Table 3.1, each row shows a test of change, the process measure we used to evaluate whether that change resulted in improvement, and key findings. Each subsequent row shows how the test was refined in the next PDSA cycle. Some problems identified through our testing have been solved, and some still require further testing to understand how best to engage parents in educational interventions. Other problems have not yet been addressed but will be included in future

Table 3.1. PDSA Ramp to Empower Parents to Manage Minor Illnesses

Test	Process Measure	Key Findings
1. Nurse education (including photographs and hands-on demonstrations) during newborn visits about top conditions accounting for nonurgent ED visits	Parent feedback at follow-up phone call Nurse feedback	Parents valued information Parents wanted something to take home and reference later Nurses had trouble reaching every infant due to time constraints Newborn visit was very long
2. Education adapted into a slideshow presentation with voice-over, medical assistant (MA) started the slideshow on the computer in the exam room at the end of the intake process	Parent feedback at end of visit MA feedback Sample 1 day/week to count how many saw the slideshow	Parents valued information When toddler siblings were present, parents had trouble paying attention to the video Parents wanted reference material to take home Less than half of parents were being shown the slideshow because speakers in some exam rooms had been stolen Slideshow only in English
3. New speakers purchased for some exam rooms and tethered to desk, test repeated	Parent feedback at end of visit MA feedback Sample 1 day/week to count how many saw the slideshow	Same as above, except this time almost all English-speaking families viewed the slideshow
4. Slideshow converted to YouTube video and link was texted to 10 families at the end of visit, in addition to showing the slideshow at beginning of visit	Follow-up phone call to parents 1 week after visit to ask if they had watched video at home or shared with family members	No families had watched the video at home or shared with family members—did not feel they needed to watch it a second time
5. Newborn coordinator texted YouTube video to families in advance of newborn visit instead of showing slideshow at visit	Follow-up phone call to parents 1 week after visit to ask if they had watched video at home or shared with family members	No families had watched the video at home or shared with family members—forgot about it or did not have time
6. Tangible cards with a Quick Response (QR) code linking to the video and clinic Wi-Fi information distributed to families at newborn visit check-in	Parent feedback at end of visit	Families looked at cards but most did not know how to use a QR code

(Continued)

Table 3.1. Continued

Test	Process Measure	Key Findings
7. New cards distributed with links instead of QR codes	Parent feedback at end of visit Follow-up phone call to parents 1 week after visit to ask if they had watched video at home	Families looked at cards but did not watch video
8. Several iterations of cards to make link simpler and make cards more engaging	Parent feedback at end of visit Follow-up phone call to parents 1 week after visit to ask if they had watched video at home	Test currently in progress

tests. For example, once effective and engaging materials are developed for the English-speaking population, we will translate materials and test interventions with non-English speaking families.

Progress, Challenges, and Future Directions

As shown in our control charts (Figures 3.1–3.3), we have achieved our goal for timely newborn visits but have yet to achieve our goal related to reduction in nonurgent ED visits. Although we strongly believe that an improvement science approach is appropriate to apply to this problem, there have been some challenges of using improvement science in this context. First, in any improvement work, organizational culture must be considered. In our specific project, because we were working across sectors to affect complex community health problems, we needed to build relationships before testing changes. This included developing a common language among the participants in improvement, agreeing upon goals, and identifying feasible changes within each sector to build confidence that change could be achieved with existing resources. Lines of communication were opened through face-to-face meetings, telephone meetings, and exchange of contact information for real-time questions when serving families. Strategies to enhance cross-sector communication included review of case studies with opportunities for each organization to contribute their expertise, as well as exercises in which each organization developed and shared process maps. These activities helped identify process steps that intersected with other organizations' work and to help each organization understand the contributions and challenges of other organizations that supported similar client groups.

Second, when addressing the true root causes of suboptimal healthcare use in a low-income community, large-scale changes, such as policy changes and building trust in the community, are likely needed. These changes are often slow and difficult to measure and are not as conducive to the application of rapid, small-scale tests of change on which improvement science is built.

Third, it is difficult to establish process measures for some of the more subjective changes that may be needed to move our outcome measures. For example, social isolation is plausibly a root cause of going to the ED when worried about an infant's health instead of consulting a trusted family member or professional. However, measuring mothers' sense of social isolation in a community is difficult in the context of a rapid PDSA cycle, as using existing validated questionnaires (which are very long) is not practical, so pursuing this area would mean extra steps to select a feasible measure. If this sense of social isolation is reduced through our interventions, it is still several steps removed from the outcome of interest, and the primary outcome measure would not be expected to change quickly in a way that can be directly linked to the intervention. This is an example of a measure that may be helpful for small-scale testing but would not be adopted as an overall project measure at the outset. As other barriers are solved through iterative testing, this is an example of a measure (and change area) that could be explored to see if a remaining gap between observed and desired ED and newborn primary care visit rates could be narrowed by addressing it.

Finally, time series analysis can identify temporal associations but cannot demonstrate causation. In a complex, community-wide system, many changes are often happening at once, and it is difficult to know which ones contributed to the results. Furthermore, it is not practical to test one change at a time when there is a strong theory that multiple changes are needed. PDSA ramps can give good confidence that a particular strategy is contributing to the desired result. However, results must be interpreted with an in-depth knowledge of changes that are happening across all parts of the system and careful documentation of the timing of interventions. As an example, in Figure 3.3, a significant decrease in ED visits was observed around the time our work began, but we know that the PPC clinic had just begun accepting walk-in ill visits at that time. Because the walk-in policy was associated with a decrease in ED visits for the general population of PPC patients of all ages from all neighborhoods, we can be fairly confident that this decrease was due to the walk-in policy and not any of our Avondale- and newborn-specific interventions.

Future directions include spread of successful interventions related to timing of the newborn visit to other health centers serving Avondale newborns. We will also continue iterative testing to further reduce ED visits for CCHMC clinic infants, guided by our key driver diagram. Once effective interventions have been developed in this group, we will spread these strategies to other health centers. Because local context is important in introducing and adapting new practices, PDSA cycles will be required in these new settings to achieve improvement of outcomes in ways that are appropriate for the workflow and patient population in these health centers. Our strategy for closing the gap at scale in our local population is the continual learning in one health center coupled with a spread strategy that supports adaptation of successful changes to customize to the other health centers and their organizational partners.

References

U.S. Census Bureau; 2011–2015 American Community Survey 5-Year Estimates, Table ZCTA5 45229; generated by Courtney Brown; using American FactFinder; https://factfinder.census.gov/faces/nav/jsf/pages/index.xhtml; (December 16, 2016)

Anderson, J. B., Beekman, R. H., Kugler, J. D., Rosenthal, G. L., Jenkins, K. J., Klitzner, T. S., ... Lannon, C. (2014). Use of a learning network to improve variation in interstage weight gain after the Norwood operation. *Congenital Heart Disease, 9*(6), 512–520.

Bernstein, H. H., Spino, C., Finch, S., Wasserman, R., Slora, E., Lalama, C., ... McCormick, M. C. (2007). Decision-making for postpartum discharge of 4300 mothers and their healthy infants: The Life Around Newborn Discharge study. *Pediatrics, 120*(2), e391–e400.

Bigham, M. T., Amato, R., Bondurrant, P., Fridriksson, J., Krawczeski, C. D., Raake, J., ... Brilli, R. J. (2009). Ventilator-associated pneumonia in the pediatric intensive care unit: Characterizing the problem and implementing a sustainable solution. *Journal of Pediatrics, 154*(4), 582–587.

Brinkman, W. B., Hartl Majcher, J., Poling, L. M., Shi, G., Zender, M., Sucharew, H., ... Epstein, J. N. (2013). Shared decision-making to improve attention-deficit hyperactivity disorder care. *Patient Education and Counseling, 93*(1), 95–101.

Brousseau, D. C., Hoffmann, R. G., Nattinger, A. B., Flores, G., Zhang, Y., & Gorelick, M. (2007). Quality of primary care and subsequent pediatric emergency department utilization. *Pediatrics, 119*(6), 1131–1138.

Chi, D., Momany, E., & Jones, M. (2013). An explanatory model of factors related to well baby visits by age three years for Medicaid-enrolled infants: A retrospective cohort study. *BMC Pediatrics, 13*, 158.

Forrest, C. B., Margolis, P., Seid, M., & Colletti, R. B. (2014). PEDSnet: How a prototype pediatric learning health system is being expanded into a national network. *Health Affairs, 33*(7), 1171–1177.

Goyal, N. K., Fager, C., & Lorch, S. A. (2011). Adherence to discharge guidelines for late-preterm newborns. *Pediatrics, 128*(1), 62–71.

Langley, G., Nolan, K., Norman, C., Provost, L., & Nolan, T. (1996). *The improvement guide: A practical approach to enhancing organizational performance* (2nd ed.). San Francisco, CA: Jossey-Bass.

Lannon, C., Brack, V., Stuart, J., Caplow, M., McNeill, A., Bordley, W. C., & Margolis, P. (1995). What mothers say about why poor children fall behind on immunizations: A summary of focus groups in North Carolina. *Archives of Pediatrics and Adolescent Medicine, 149*(10), 1070–1075.

Lansky, A., Barfield, W. D., Marchi, K. S., Egerter, S. A., Galbraith, A. A., & Braveman, P. A. (2006). Early postnatal care among healthy newborns in 19 states: Pregnancy risk assessment monitoring system, 2000. *Maternal and Child Health Journal, 10*(3), 277–284.

Meara, E., Kotagal, U. R., Atherton, H. D., & Lieu, T. A. (2004). Impact of early newborn discharge legislation and early follow-up visits on infant outcomes in a state Medicaid population. *Pediatrics, 113*(6), 1619–1627.

Muething, S. E., Goudie, A., Schoettker, P. J., Donnelly, L. F., Goodfriend, M. A., Bracke, T. M., ... Kotagal, U. R. (2012). Quality improvement initiative to reduce serious safety events and improve patient safety culture. *Pediatrics, 130*(2), e423–e431.

National Center for Children in Poverty. (2011). *Researchers: Detroit, Cleveland, Cincinnati, Buffalo, Milwaukee lead nation in child poverty* [Press release].

Nicholas, S. W., Jean-Louis, B., Ortiz, B., Northridge, M., Shoemaker, K., Vaughan, R., ... Hutchinson, V. (2005). Addressing the childhood asthma crisis in Harlem: The Harlem Children's Zone Asthma Initiative. *American Journal of Public Health, 95*(2), 245–249.

O'Donnell, H. C., Trachtman, R. A., Islam, S., & Racine, A. D. (2014). Factors associated with timing of first outpatient visit after newborn hospital discharge. *Academic Pediatrics, 14*(1), 77–83.

Provost, L. P., & Murray, S. (2011). *The health care data guide: Learning from data for improvement.* San Francisco, CA: Jossey-Bass.

Shakib, J., Buchi, K., Smith, E., Korgenski, K., & Young, P. C. (2015). Timing of initial well-child visit and readmissions of newborns. *Pediatrics, 135*(3), 469–474.

Spielman, S., Golembeski, C., Northridge, M., Vaughan, R., Swaner, R., Jean-Louis, B., ... Sclar, E. (2006). Interdisciplinary planning for healthier communities: Findings from the Harlem Children's Zone Asthma Initiative. *Journal of the American Planning Association, 72*(1), 100–108.

Suruda, A., Burns, T. J., Knight, S., & Dean, J. M. (2005). Health insurance, neighborhood income, and emergency department usage by Utah children 1996–1998. *BMC Health Services Research, 5*(1), 29.

Tomashek, K. M., Shapiro-Mendoza, C. K., Weiss, J., Kotelchuck, M., Barfield, W., Evans, S., ... Declercq, E. (2006). Early discharge among late preterm and term newborns and risk of neonatal morbidity. *Seminars in Perinatology, 30*(2), 61–68.

Van Berckelaer, A., Mitra, N., & Pati, S. (2011). Predictors of well child care adherence over time in a cohort of urban Medicaid-eligible infants. *BMC Pediatrics, 11*, 36.

Zlotnick, C. (2007). Community-versus individual-level indicators to identify pediatric health care need. *Journal of Urban Health, 84*(1), 45–59.

COURTNEY M. BROWN, MD, MSc, *is an assistant professor of pediatrics at the University of Cincinnati School of Medicine in the Division of General and Community Pediatrics at Cincinnati Children's Hospital Medical Center and is an affiliate faculty member in the James M. Anderson Center for Health Systems Excellence.*

ROBERT S. KAHN, MD, MPH, *is a professor of pediatrics at the University of Cincinnati School of Medicine in the Division of General and Community Pediatrics at Cincinnati Children's Hospital Medical Center and is associate chair of community health in the Department of Pediatrics.*

NEERA K. GOYAL, MD, MSc, *is an assistant professor of pediatrics at the University of Cincinnati School of Medicine in the Division of Neonatology and the Division of Hospital Medicine at Cincinnati Children's Hospital Medical Center and is an affiliate faculty member in the James M. Anderson Center for Health Systems Excellence.*

Inkelas, M., Bowie, P., & Guirguis, L. (2017). Improvement for a community population: the magnolia community initiative. In C. A. Christie, M. Inkelas & S. Lemire (Eds.), *Improvement Science in Evaluation: Methods and Uses. New Directions for Evaluation, 153*, 51–64.

4

Improvement for a Community Population: The Magnolia Community Initiative

Moira Inkelas, Patricia Bowie, Lila Guirguis

Abstract

Improvement science is a promising approach to changing practice in complex community systems, which are characterized by many independent organizations with separate missions, services, and outcomes. This example shows how a network of diverse organizations is using iterative learning to come up with promising ideas, test and prototype these ideas, and spread and sustain what is found to work. The Magnolia Community Initiative (MCI) is an approach for improving population well-being at a community scale, as a voluntary network of 70+ government, nonprofit, and for-profit organizations supporting a population of over 100,000 people. Diverse organizations from multiple service sectors strive to work as a system by aligning and improving resources to change conditions and outcomes for local families that they could not achieve by working alone. MCI adopted an approach that combined knowledge of what to change to improve child and family well-being, based on theory and on the expertise of organizations that comprise the network, with knowledge of how to change within a complex system, using improvement science. © 2017 Wiley Periodicals, Inc., and the American Evaluation Association.

T he Magnolia Community Initiative (MCI) is an approach for improving population well-being at a community scale (Bowie, 2011). MCI is a voluntary network of about 70 organizations that came together with the vision of 35,000 children living in the neighborhoods within a 500-block catchment area breaking records of success in their education, health, quality of nurturing care, and economic stability. Partner organizations include the Los Angeles County Chief Executive Office (CEO) and multiple county departments including social services, child protection, and child support services; regional publicly funded organizations responsible for geographic populations of children such as the school district, Special Supplemental Nutrition Program for Women, Infants, and Children (WIC), and child care resource and referral; health care, including several federally qualified health centers; early care and education programs; home visiting programs; family support programs; and economic services and supports.

A holistic model of the formation, maintenance, and improvement of health and well-being guides MCI actions. There is growing evidence that wellness behaviors—which include healthy habits as well as consistently following care plans for chronic conditions and health risks—begin in childhood and are heavily shaped by family and neighborhood environments (Hertzman & Power, 2003). Rather than focus on a specific health concern, or several health concerns, MCI focused on aspects of well-being that are the foundation for health, learning, and civic participation across the life course, such as social connections and resilience, because these are critical capacities for thriving in the face of life challenges (Hertzman & Power, 2003). As a network, MCI partners have the potential to influence neighborhood context, family conditions, and home environment, which are known in combination to influence child health and well-being. Within the MCI catchment area, about 65% of local children live in poverty, 35% are overweight, 70% are not proficient in reading by third grade, and 40% will fail to graduate from high school. One-third of adults have less than a ninth-grade education, and 54% have less than high school education. With a holistic vision of health determinants, partners sought to create a systemic approach that could improve conditions and outcomes for a local population of children and families.

The following sections describe why MCI sought to apply improvement science to achieve its goals, based on insights into how population-focused initiatives have fallen short in the past, what elements of complex systems have been the most challenging, and what is considered necessary to achieve sustainable improvement at the scale of a population. A description of what MCI sought to accomplish is followed by a description of how MCI introduced measurement, rapid learning, adjusting and refinement of changes into the collective work of partner organizations. The chapter concludes with opportunities and some challenges in using improvement science to achieve community-wide outcomes.

NEW DIRECTIONS FOR EVALUATION • DOI: 10.1002/ev

Working as a System

The partnering agencies committed to a shared vision and specific goals, with the understanding that each organization would retain its own unique agenda and strategies. The partners focused on changes that they could make without additional resources, beyond limited grant-funded support of a small management team (MCI network staff). The partners believed that no single intervention or even combination of evidence-based interventions would suffice to achieve their population-level goals of health, education, nurturing care, and economic stability. Instead, the partners aimed to align their actions by following a shared theory of human development and family support. At the most basic level, the partners needed a process of introducing and testing changes together, as a system, rather than only in the traditional way of introducing new programs or services within their own organizations. For example, reliable linkage of clients between organizations requires action from the referring and the receiving organization so multiple organizations need to collaborate in learning what changes will produce the result that they seek. The partners also realized that a community system is dynamic with constant change in programs, services, and policies. An appreciation of the behavior of complex systems led to the insight that a community system will never be permanently "fixed." Therefore, relying on the successful introduction of time-limited interventions or programs, such as home visiting, was not the sustainable approach that they sought. Instead, there was a need for an approach to change that could produce ongoing innovation and improvement that could respond to changing practice and policy environments.

Focus on Scale

The emphasis of MCI is aligning multiple sectors and programs so that they function as a system of care for families at the scale necessary to change outcomes in a geographic population, not only for an individual family or for a small subgroup of the population. The ability to introduce changes at scale was thought to be essential for achieving population-level outcomes by sustaining the innovations and improvements that the network produced (Bowie, 2011). None of the partner organizations had previously sought to change an outcome at a population scale; instead, they had each focused on programs for the clients that they had at any given time. As a result, MCI needed an approach to change that focused on scale from the outset, realizing that programs that are perfected for small samples, specific organizations, or in controlled conditions often fail to work at the scale for which they are actually intended. MCI needed a learning method that examined the context for implementation so that the ultimate set of processes would work as intended at the necessary scale (Moen, 2002; Rogers, 2003).

Aligning Multiple Sector Focus on Outcomes

A current trend in multiple service sectors including health, education, early education, and social services such as home visiting and child protection is greater accountability for achieving family and child outcomes. The Affordable Care Act (ACA) is an example of federal policy creating new incentives for population, prevention, and wellness strategies in health and mental health. This transition of health, social, and education sectors from a focus on outputs (such as volume served) to quality and outcomes creates an opportunity for alignment, but it requires a new production model with insight into, and the ability to change, the underlying factors that influence outcomes. This implies a learning method that offers data on outcomes as well as on the mechanisms for changing those outcomes and a method that enables organizations to discover ways of being mutually reinforcing. Organizations often perceive that they are being held to outcomes without being given the knowledge base, resources, or partners to achieve them. Additionally, most partner organizations in the MCI network had, at best, annual measures of process and outcome, lacking measurement in real time or disaggregated to the level of specific settings or providers.

Focusing on a Continuum of Family-Focused Supports and Services

In forming MCI, partners agreed on what was most important to change. MCI sought to change institutional approaches from delivering isolated human services to providing care that is preventive, holistic, and responsive to each client. The MCI vision was to raise family well-being as a topic with all clients, regardless of the organization's primary mission. This required a common language so that providers and staff from different disciplines would understand the core practice concepts and an innovation and improvement approach that would help providers and staff apply these concepts within the particular context of an organization. For example, MCI embraced empathy as a core philosophy for improving the quality and responsiveness of the services and supports that network partners provide and to build relationships between residents to reduce social isolation and increase community belonging. MCI also developed a "belonging" campaign to assist providers and staff to understand how belonging is a network concept that informs their daily work, just as a neighborhood campaign sought to increase a sense of belonging among residents and actions following from it. The spread of empathy and belonging, as well as other core concepts, required not only a common language but also a coaching process that would help providers and staff translate these concepts into their daily practice.

Introduction of Improvement Science

A community system such as MCI has a need for change management that supports several related goals at the same time: developing new concepts at a community level such as empathy and belonging, creating new processes such as seamless linkage and warm handoffs across a network of partners, and improving existing evidence-informed practices (such as depression screening, financial screening) so that care is more reliable (consistent). MCI sought to introduce improvement methods to support problem solving, encourage testing of innovative ideas, and support data collection to provide feedback on the effectiveness of new ideas and strategies. Few partners had any prior experience with improvement science. MCI introduced the Model for Improvement (Langley et al., 2009) as the overarching change strategy to support collective actions across the network.

Figure 4.1 shows improvement science as a core strategy in MCI's theory of change, displayed in a driver diagram format that is common in improvement science (Bennett & Provost, 2015; Langley et al., 2009). Process improvement is a driver, coupled with accountable leadership focused on population outcomes, supporting the human element of change, and measuring and sharing data. These elements are considered to be part of successful improvement approaches (Langley et al., 2009); they are listed separately in the MCI driver diagram but are each considered as vital elements of change management. The following paragraphs describe how improvement science has introduced regular actionable data, learning cycles, and learning from variation into the MCI network.

Regular Actionable Data

Partners received monthly reports on key measures, with time series displays that show their organization's rates on processes that the network has sought to optimize. Monthly measures in time series format enabled partners to see whether changes that they introduced were reflected as improvement in the measures and to assess the reliability (consistency) of their processes. Partners introduced brief, anonymous surveys of small samples of their clients after visits/encounters. This enabled partners to monitor their progress by reviewing their own data monthly, using small learning cycles to test improvements and then gauge their impact using the time series display. Few partners had viewed data in time series format, or with monthly periodicity, and none had regular client feedback on care processes outside of annual client satisfaction surveys that enabled partners to know if changes were leading to improvements.

MCI also created a population dashboard to show MCI partners real-time, monthly progress on process of care measures (Figure 4.2). This is a fundamental improvement science method for connecting people to shared accountability for results and a common change process. On the dashboard, monthly measures show the levels of performance, that is, which processes are happening consistently or not. The time series charts also segment the rates by service to make it possible to learn from variation in practice between sectors in the network. This regular reporting by sector helps

NEW DIRECTIONS FOR EVALUATION • DOI: 10.1002/ev

Figure 4.1. Magnolia Community Initiative Driver Diagram

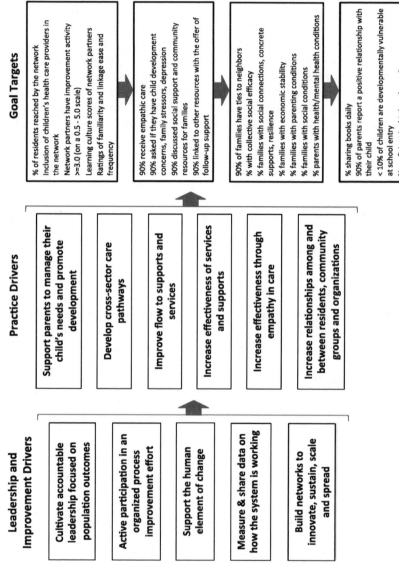

Leadership and Improvement Drivers

- Cultivate accountable leadership focused on population outcomes
- Active participation in an organized process improvement effort
- Support the human element of change
- Measure & share data on how the system is working
- Build networks to innovate, sustain, scale and spread

Practice Drivers

- Support parents to manage their child's needs and promote development
- Develop cross-sector care pathways
- Improve flow to supports and services
- Increase effectiveness of services and supports
- Increase effectiveness through empathy in care
- Increase relationships among and between residents, community groups and organizations

Goal Targets

- % of residents reached by the network
- Inclusion of children's health care providers in the network
- Network partners have improvement activity >=3.0 (on a 0.5 - 5.0 scale)
- Learning culture scores of network partners
- Ratings of familiarity and linkage ease and frequency

- 90% receive empathic care
- 90% asked if they have child development concerns, family stressors, depression
- 90% discussed social support and community resources for families
- 90% linked to other resources with the offer of follow-up support

---

- 90% of families have ties to neighbors
- % with collective social efficacy
- % families with social connections, concrete supports, resilience
- % families with economic stability
- % families with parenting conditions
- % families with social conditions
- % parents with health/mental health conditions

- % sharing books daily
- 90% of parents report a positive relationship with their child
- < 10% of children are developmentally vulnerable at school entry
- % proficient in third grade reading

Figure 4.2. Magnolia Community Initiative Population Dashboard

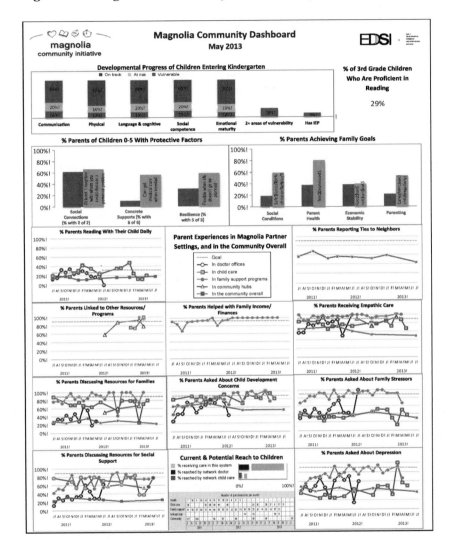

organizations see variation that enables them to learn from each other (Bowie & Inkelas, 2014; Inkelas & Bowie, 2014). The dashboard reflects other principles of improvement science, displaying not only the real-time processes but also the intermediate outcomes (family behaviors and family conditions) and the ultimate outcomes (child well-being, measured at kindergarten and third grade). These family and child outcomes are measured at the level of the population through periodic community samples, whereas the monthly measures come from clients who interact with the partner organizations. Reflecting the improvement science emphasis on scale, the MCI dashboard also shows the percentage of the local population of families that the partner organizations are reaching. This measure shows the partners that even optimal performance on the process measures on the dashboard will not alter the family and child outcomes on the upper part of the dashboard until the network is extending these processes to a large proportion of the local community. This is a constant reminder that working at scale means more than introducing an effective program within an organization. Instead, it means having a robust network that reaches everyone in the target population and extends the necessary services and supports to them.

Learning Cycles

Periodic meetings of partners, and coaching support during and between meetings, have enabled the partners to learn how to design and test changes. Frontline staff and providers receive coaching in the Model for Improvement and guidance in how to set aims and create tests of change (Plan–Do–Study–Act [PDSA] cycles). New processes for the partners included engaging frontline staff and providers in crafting small learning cycles, providing regular data to these individuals, and helping them to set aside time to plan and carry out learning cycles. These processes were not part of the organizational culture in most MCI partner organizations. In addition to ongoing exposure to improvement methods, MCI followed a "lead user" approach (von Hippel, 1986) in which partner organizations with greater management and staff readiness for improvement methods could model the process for other organizations.

Exhibit 4.1 offers one example of how introduction of improvement science supported a change process within MCI. In this example, eligibility staff from three public social services agencies introduced several process changes using iterative learning methods. Their rationale for this change was that effective linkage and client flow are essential for meeting the unique needs and mobilizing the unique strengths of each family. These agencies perceived value of acting as a "one-stop network" in which they could take advantage of the large volume of families that they encounter to link them with other resources that they need, such as economic stability resources, or support for depression. MCI offered partners a database of local services and supports, but partners needed to develop reliable processes for eliciting concerns among clients and then linking clients to those services. Such linkage processes are consistent with the mission of county departments and the goals of eligibility workers, but they are not responsibilities of these staff. For this reason, it was necessary for workers to learn how they might incorporate these processes into their daily workflow without reducing their productivity, upsetting clients, or creating client expectations for response that the MCI network was not capable of providing.

As they began their learning cycles, the agency staff received organizing support from middle managers in their agencies and from a service

Exhibit 4.1. Example of Cross-Agency Improvement

MCI network organizations work from a driver diagram that asks the question of what changes will lead to improvement, rather than prescribing a detailed intervention that partners would be expected to implement. The emphasis on the change idea rather than a specified protocol enabled individuals from several agencies to work as a team to consider what they were trying to achieve and how they could put that new concept into practice.

Eligibility staff from several Los Angeles County Departments sought to introduce a new process into their daily practice. Public Social Services helps individuals apply for subsidized health insurance, and cash assistance, and nutrition support (Special Nutrition Assistance Program, SNAP). Child Support Services helps absent parents work out how they will financially support their children, and helps single parents get the financial support that they are owed for their children. Children and Family Services provides protective services, which includes some prevention support for families at risk of abuse and neglect, as well as emergency response, and foster care services.

These individuals came together to consider a response to a recent survey of community members that revealed that 20% of parents of young children report depression and that only 50% were asked by a health care provider in the past year about depression The team identified the MCI driver of improving flow to services and supports as a way that they could contribute. Each of the participating agencies has a large volume of clients coming through each day, so as large reach organizations, these agencies could have a large impact in the community with any process that they introduce into daily practice. At the same time, the staff can only make small changes to their daily practice given their full workloads. The agency staff sought a way of eliciting depression risk so that their clients could receive support in a timely way from other partners in the network.

The individuals considered their readiness to implement a change. Some team members were ready to get started while other team members were motivated to contribute but were not ready to introduce a change. The team members decided that they needed answers to several questions: how do we raise the topic? How do we reliably fit this question into our workflow? And are we confident that our hand-offs will work if the client wants support?

Their first PDSA predicted that clients would not mind being asked about sadness or depression. The team started with each of the two ready staff members each asking one client each. Rather than spend extended time planning and deciding what the ideal way to ask the question might be, the team started by asking a question from the PHQ-2 (Patient Health Questionnaire), is a well known depression screener was an easy way to get started. The first test found that the two clients did not mind being asked, but the question seemed too formal and seemed out of place in the part of the encounter in which it was posed. Staff members involved in the first test were skilled with establishing rapport with clients but thought that they and other staff might be more successful if they could do this more conversationally. Their intent was not to screen for depression for purposes of treatment but instead to get a sense of the client's needs so they can link the person to an organization that can properly triage them, and then either provide resources or put them in touch with a network partner that could meet their needs.

The agency staff began measuring their rates of eliciting client concerns in the post-encounter client survey that multiple MCI partners were implementing to understand client experiences. The staff did a lot of small testing in the first several months that resulted in no measurable change in their process. This was expected as they were doing focused learning with only one or two clients in each small learning cycle. Once they had completed enough tests of the process to feel confident that they had a workable process, they introduced it as a protocol for all clients. They then used the routine measurement, using the voice of their clients to gauge the extent to which clients were experiencing the process that the staff had sought to implement. Within several months, staff was asking about depression in at least 80% of encounters and ultimately achieved their goal of 90%. Staff also achieved a similar rate for the measure of discussing resources for social support in the community. Both processes have sustained over time.

NEW DIRECTIONS FOR EVALUATION • DOI: 10.1002/ev

integration agency within Los Angeles County. These middle managers ensured that staff had a small amount of time set aside weekly for planning the learning cycles, and they met regularly with the team to help them organize their testing. Several improvement coaches from the MCI network provided monthly data from the anonymous surveys completed by a small number of clients after their encounters with these agency staff. During monthly network meetings that included these improvement coaches and staff from about 15 other MCI partner organizations, the agency staff received guidance on how to plan and implement small learning cycles and how to interpret their monthly time series data.

Figure 4.3 lists several of the sequential learning cycles that agency staff used to iterate toward processes that they could reliably implement and sustain over time. For example, the first learning cycles focused on acceptability of a new process for the staff and the clients. Later learning cycles focused on optimizing the process in terms of finding the most concise way of asking and addressing the questions, identifying the best time during the encounter to include this content, and calling a small number of clients to learn if they had actually made contact with the organization they were referred to. Staff also used learning cycles to ensure that introducing the new processes would not adversely affect their workflow and responsibilities, as measured by their ability to meet productivity standards in terms of total daily encounters. Figure 4.3 also shows the time series run charts for two processes that the staff sought to implement, beginning before any learning cycles had been introduced and extending for about 24 months after the staff sought to implement these processes in all encounters. The staff maintained these processes at a high level of reliability with occasional lapses due to staff turnover. One of these measures (asking about depression) appears on the MCI dashboard (Figure 4.2).

As another example, a subgroup of partners began using improvement science to help families introduce positive and consistent routines in their daily life. This cross-sector group included professionals from child care programs, reading groups, and family support programs. The group sought to help families identify and address barriers to a specific daily routine of parent–child book sharing. The partners created reading diaries and run charts to help parents track how often they were able to follow a home reading routine, share their challenges and ideas for improvement with other parents and then test changes in their home routine that could get them closer to their goal of daily book sharing. This group of partners has used improvement science at two levels: first, in their own work as they test the format of reading logs and their own roles as champions of family behavior change, and second in a simple process of learning cycles and measurement for families so that families can learn from their own attempts and from other families as well. Toward this end, families receive their own data and that of other parents as a whole. Preliminary results show increased rates of reading among participating families.

Figure 4.3. Improvement Example

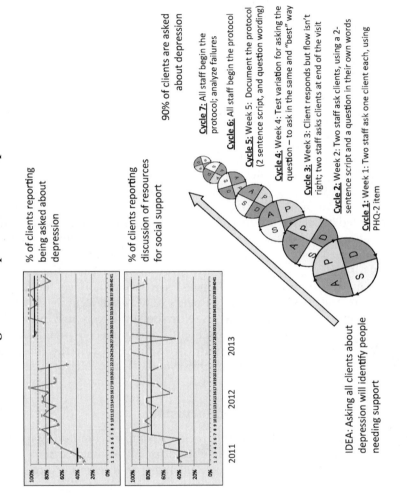

% of clients reporting being asked about depression

% of clients reporting discussion of resources for social support

90% of clients are asked about depression

Cycle 7: All staff begin the protocol; analyze failures

Cycle 6: All staff begin the protocol

Cycle 5: Week 5: Document the protocol (2 sentence script, and question wording)

Cycle 4: Week 4: Test variation for asking the question – to ask in the same and "best" way

Cycle 3: Week 3: Client responds but flow isn't right; two staff asks clients at end of the visit

Cycle 2: Week 2: Two staff ask clients, using a 2-sentence script and a question in their own words

Cycle 1: Week 1: Two staff ask one client each, using PHQ-2 item

IDEA: Asking all clients about depression will identify people needing support

2011   2012   2013

Learning from Variation

The MCI theory of change emphasizes a peer production approach that reflects key principles in improvement science (Margolis & Seid, 2014). The intent is for each partner to contribute to the overall goal of the network by offering services and supports based on its unique capabilities and to make the collective more than the sum of its parts by sharing unique disciplinary expertise related to working with families with other partners in the network, in planning new processes in areas such as empathy, linkage protocols, and care processes. This requires system thinking where the partners determine as a group what changes all of the partners could make that would create a more consistent, seamless, and effective experience for people who access services from one or more of the partners. Comparing data across organizations sparked this system thinking and also spurred some partners that were less confident about some of the care processes to begin testing them after seeing that other partner organizations like their own had managed to introduce them.

The MCI network sought to use monthly improvement meetings to encourage organizations with a particular interest and expertise in a change idea, and with their leader's commitment to seeing through a learning process, to take the lead on different types of innovations that ultimately would be adopted by all network partners. The expectation is that there are different lead users for different MCI core concepts (such as linkage, empathy, and others). This "lead user" approach enables organizations that are more ready for a change to make that idea work in practice and then share how it was done with others (von Hippel, 1986), which follows the facilitative diffusion strategies described by Rogers (2003) and Deming (2000). This is important in a network where the drivers are largely new processes for organizations, rather than improvements to existing core practices. For example, the elicitation and referral process developed by the three county departments led to improvements in several other partner organizations.

Conclusion

Achieving better population outcomes in a complex community system will often require increasing the reliability of intended practice across a range of organizations, as well as developing and spreading innovations that can close the gap between knowledge and practice. The MCI theory of change calls for partner organizations to work collectively on key drivers of child and family outcomes. Each of these drivers require innovation in areas of practice where little is known or published (requiring concept development and initial testing) as well as reliability and spread strategies for areas of practice where there is good science and existing models of successful practice but low local performance. At any given time, partners have a need for learning methods at each of these different phases of implementation. For example, some MCI partners are creating promising ideas based on theory and user needs (such as promoting the concept of "belonging" across the network), and at the same time, others are creating small-scale versions of ideas to increase degree of belief (such as increasing screening and referral processes for network supports within client encounters), whereas most partners are working on a spread goal of using empathy in all client encounters. Improvement science offers methods that apply across this continuum of knowledge, from innovation, to implementation under varying conditions, to scale and spread.

Despite their promise, improvement methods such as the use of real-time data in time series format at the level of frontline service are not commonly used in community-based organizations. Supporting improvement in a large diverse network means attending to different capabilities among the partners. This means having resources to help organizations learn the process and support it at all organizational levels: leadership, management and frontline providers and staff. MCI's infrastructure for improvement support is continuously evolving. For example, MCI developed a networkwide capacity-building strategy that introduces select managers from partner organizations to participate in an annual fellowship series that familiarize managers with MCI content as well as uses of data and learning cycles for improvement. This may be an effective and sustainable way of infusing improvement methods into partner organizations.

It is worth noting that MCI is one prototype of how organizations from multiple sectors can work together as a network to improve outcomes for a population, using a common vision, network theory, and improvement science. Future experience will answer key questions about the use of improvement science to achieve a population outcome, such as: Will leaders of a critical mass of partnering organizations commit the necessary leadership and time? What impact will staff turnover have on the depth of improvement skills in the partnering agencies? Will public health or other regional organizations in health or other sectors take ownership of any of the time series measurement and improvement coaching responsibilities? Will innovation and improvement methods introduce the right set of process changes at a threshold of reliability that is necessary to influence health outcomes?

In summary, MCI provides an example of how improvement science offers practical strategies that can be applied in cross-sector population-focused efforts. Improvement science has been successfully applied to introduce evidence-based interventions into daily practice. To achieve population outcomes, there is a need to integrate expertise in how to change within a complex system with knowledge of what to change. In this way, a network of organizations acts rather than plans its way into a new system. As evaluators partner with communities to learn how networks of independent partners can function as a system, there is a growing need to introduce processes that enable communities to create, design, and test better concepts for practice. Improvement science offers one such organized approach to learning.

References

Bennett, B., & Provost, L. (2015, July). What's your theory? *Quality Progress*. Retrieved from www.qualityprogress.com

Bowie, P. (2011). *Getting to scale: The elusive goal. Magnolia Place Community Initiative*. Seattle, WA: Casey Family Programs.

Bowie, P., & Inkelas, M. (2014). Using data to drive change in complex community systems. In N. Cytron, K. L. S. Pettit, & G. T. Kingsley (Eds.), *What counts: Harnessing data for America's communities* (pp. 378–395). San Francisco, CA: Federal Reserve Bank of San Francisco; Washington, DC: Urban Institute.

Deming, W. E. (2000). *The new economics for industry, government, education* (2nd ed.). Boston, MA: MIT Press.

Hertzman, C., & Power, C. (2003). Health and human development: Understandings from life-course research. *Developmental Neuropsychology, 24*(2–3), 719–744.

Inkelas, M., & Bowie, P. (2014). The Magnolia Community Initiative: The importance of measurement in improving community well-being. *Community Investments, 26*(1), 18–24.

Langley, G., Moen, R. D., Nolan, K. M., Nolan, T. W., Norman, C. L., & Provost, L. P. (2009). *The improvement guide: A practical guide to enhancing organizational performance* (2nd ed.). San Francisco, CA: Jossey-Bass.

Margolis, P. A., & Seid, M. (2014). Engagement, peer production, and the learning healthcare system. *JAMA Pediatrics, 168*(3), 201–202.

Moen, R. (2002). *A guide to idealized design*. Cambridge, MA: Institute for Healthcare Improvement.

Rogers, E. (2003). *Diffusion of innovations* (5th ed.). New York, NY: Simon and Schuster.

von Hippel, E. (1986). Lead users: A source of novel product concepts. *Manage Science, 32*(7), 791–805.

MOIRA INKELAS is associate professor in the Department of Health Policy and Management in the UCLA Fielding School of Public Health and assistant director of the Center for Healthier Children, Families and Communities.

PATRICIA BOWIE is affiliated with the UCLA Center for Healthier Children, Families and Communities and a partner in the design and implementation of the Magnolia Community Initiative.

LILA GUIRGUIS is the director of the Magnolia Community Initiative.

Rohanna, K. (2017). Breaking the "Adopt, Attack, Abandon" cycle: A case for improvement science in K–12 education. In C. A. Christie, M. Inkelas & S. Lemire (Eds.), *Improvement Science in Evaluation: Methods and Uses. New Directions for Evaluation, 153,* 65–77.

5

Breaking the "Adopt, Attack, Abandon" Cycle: A Case for Improvement Science in K–12 Education

Kristen Rohanna

Abstract

School reform efforts have collectively failed to find sustainable solutions to education's most pressing problems. Researchers and education practitioners have both vocalized these challenges. The difficulty of fitting proven reforms to local school contexts often leads to a cycle of "adopt, attack, and abandon." This chapter discusses the potential power of improvement science to break the cycle in education. In doing so, the research aims to understand the school leader's perspective when improvement science processes were employed at their sites. The research examined three school cases, as principals used rapid cycles of evaluations, using the improvement science PDSA model. In addition to providing a better understanding of what factors facilitate or constrain the implementation of rapid cycles of evaluation in school sites, the research offers insight into how evaluators can use improvement science methods to adapt interventions or practices to local context. © 2017 Wiley Periodicals, Inc., and the American Evaluation Association.

F inding sustainable solutions to education problems has proven problematic throughout the years. Researchers and education practitioners today are still tackling the challenges faced by those 50 years ago, particularly in the area of educational equality.

New Directions for Evaluation, no. 153, Spring 2017 © 2017 Wiley Periodicals, Inc., and the American Evaluation Association. Published online in Wiley Online Library (wileyonlinelibrary.com) • DOI: 10.1002/ev.20233

Researchers and practitioners have vocalized the hindrances that contribute to the challenges of education reform. Berliner (2002) deemed education research the "hardest science of all." In particular, he noted the difficulty of implementing or generalizing education reforms without incorporating the needs of the local context. Feuer, Towne, and Shavelson (2002) recognized that an important "challenge for the field of education is to bring diverse communities—both scientific and otherwise—together to integrate theories and empirical findings across domains, cultures, and methods" (p. 7).

Practitioners have voiced their insights as well. A former colleague of mine, who is currently a K–12 central office administrator and former high school principal, once verbalized what she believed to be a primary challenge in education reform: "We tend to adopt, attack, and abandon." She recognized that, although school administrators were quick to try to a new solution, they were not as adept at improving and modifying a strategy or intervention once it was in place. This cycle of adopting and abandoning potential solutions is particularly shattering in education due to the varied contexts in educational settings, as discussed by Berliner (2002): What works in one school might not work in another. Abandoning potentially effective strategies or interventions before adapting to the specific context makes it almost impossible to alleviate the problems facing the education system.

In response to the enduring challenges that both education researchers and practitioners have encountered, there has been a recent push to incorporate research and development (R&D) into educational improvement. The R&D paradigm provides a framework for collaborative innovation and inquiry. Researchers and practitioners work together for social innovation. As noted by Bryk, Gomez, and Grunow (2011),

> It [complex problems of practice improvement] demands new arrangements for disciplined inquiry where the work of research and practice join in a more dynamic and interactive fashion. It invites strong scholars to engage in applied R&D, but now in quite different ways in the pursuit of a science of improvement. (p. 128)

One such model in education is the Carnegie Foundation for the Advancement of Teaching improvement science model. It is built upon the science of improvement frameworks used in health care and the concept of networked improvement communities (NICs) (Bryk et al., 2011).

The intellectual foundation and core principles of improvement science are presented in Chapter 2. Of particular relevance to the present chapter is improvement science's emphasis on combining subject knowledge with profound knowledge. Subject knowledge is considered the content knowledge within a particular area, often held by practitioners and/or researchers, whereas profound knowledge is the more systematic awareness of "*how* to make changes that will result in improvement in a variety of settings" (Langley et al., 2009, p. 75). The latter can be defined "as the interplay of theories of systems, variation, knowledge, and psychology" (Deming, cited in Langley et al., 2009, p. 75).

In its practical application, this fusion of subjective and profound knowledge can be structured around Plan–Do–Study–Act (PDSA) cycles as a rapid evaluation framework to test a change of practice. PDSAs are iterative cycles of inquiry used in improvement science. During each cycle, the team develops a plan to test and predict the impact of the change (plan), conducts the test and gathers data (do), studies results and reflects (study), and acts upon the results (act). The purpose of the inquiry cycle is not only to quickly evaluate the effect of the change but also to generate new knowledge that can be used to adapt the change and try again until the change results in an improvement.

Although improvement science methods have been proven effective in numerous areas, including health care and higher education, they have yet to become prevalent in K–12 education. There are several reasons for this. First and foremost, the model, although notably effective and inspiring, can be taxing to employ because it typically requires large amounts of time, planning, and staff resources—all of which are scarce in a K–12 environment based on my experience. For example, the *90-Day Cycle Handbook* (Park & Takahashi, 2013), adapted by the Carnegie Foundation for the Advancement of Teaching from the Institute for Healthcare Improvement 90-day cycle process, gives a sound and structured methodology for improvement. However, implementing the guide's model is labor intensive, with team members participating in weekly meetings, a literature review, expert interviews, and report writing. Although this level of commitment is ideal for fostering improvement, the reality is that many education practitioners will have difficulty finding the time.

Second, because the use of improvement science models in K–12 education is a recent occurrence, existing research on the process is limited. More important, a review of the literature did not find studies connected to the "limited dosage" of these models when implemented in K–12 settings. Although improvement science responds to contextual factors when developing solutions, it tends to follow a set of processes that are applied consistently across fields and settings. Research has not yet shown whether the processes themselves can be adapted to fit the contextual factors within an organization.

Speaking directly to these challenges, the present chapter focuses on the application of the PDSA in schools by site leaders. It falls within the larger research aimed at understanding the context-responsive improvement process. Perhaps more than anyone in a district setting, site leaders understand the difficulties of implementing a "one-size-fits-all" district initiative within the context of their own schools. Thus, it is crucial to gain

NEW DIRECTIONS FOR EVALUATION • DOI: 10.1002/ev

the site leader's perspective and understand how they execute the process at the school level.

Studying the PDSA was appropriate because that was when site leaders expanded the change process to their schools, there came a crucial moment when the improvement process ran into potential challenges related to logistics, people (teachers, students), time, and resources. Ultimately, this pivotal moment could be deemed the "make or break" point in the improvement science process. The primary question guiding this chapter is: What factors facilitate or constrain the implementation of rapid cycles of evaluation in K–12 school sites?

Examining this question is important for several reasons. First, the promise of PDSA cycles in K–12 education, and improvement science more broadly, is its potential to end the "adopt, attack, and abandon" cycle. Continuous improvement and discipline inquiry cycles are nothing new in K–12 education. However, per my experience and review of more well-known inquiry models, many of them tend to be more data focused and fail to incorporate Deming's system of profound knowledge. Furthermore, they tend to lack the improvement science experimental R&D component that promotes prototyping and testing new ideas on a small scale and failing fast. It is this agile element of improvement science that offers educators and evaluators a framework to fit a potential strategy to the local context before abandoning it.

Second, improvement science's power in education evaluation is not only the disciplined inquiry to determine *what* works but also its structuring of processes for *how* to improve and continually adapt promising strategies to diverse school or classroom settings until they work. In many cases, existing education research or evaluations have identified effective strategies or interventions. However, as noted by Berliner (2002), varied school contexts and local needs can render it difficult to successfully apply and implement those strategies. Improvement science offers a practical bridge between researchers, evaluators, and practitioners. Education practitioners could engage the latest research as a resource for change ideas *after* investigating their "problem," conducting their system analysis, and developing high leverage improvement drivers; and then using PDSAs as the tool to fit evaluated and proven interventions to the local context, with the focus on adaptation versus replication,

To illustrate these promising features of PDSA cycles, the remainder of the chapter is structured in three parts. Part one presents the background and context of a study on the implementation of PDSA cycles in K–12 environments at three schools. A brief note on the methodology of the study is provided. In part two, experiences and lessons learned from implementing PDSA cycles in the three schools are shared. Informed by these, the third part of the chapter considers the implications of using PDSA for practice and evaluation.

NEW DIRECTIONS FOR EVALUATION • DOI: 10.1002/ev

The Case

Recognizing that problem solvers in a K–12 school district environment may not have the resources or time to devote to a full-scale improvement science frameworks, one California Bay Area school district implemented an initiative that explored the extent to which a more limited change process that "picks and chooses" applicable aspects of these frameworks could effectively foster change. The goal of the project was to document this context-responsive improvement process with a group of middle school principals, counselors, and central office administrators as they worked collaboratively to find solutions for increasing academic perseverance in middle school students and to determine the extent to which this process resulted in positive changes in district practices. This research was particularly interested in the rapid cycles of evaluation component.

I served as the project director for this project. Because of my interest in finding sustainable solutions and infusing innovative problem-solving thinking into district practices, I urged the district to use a collaborative approach, led by me, for addressing this problem. District data showed that the "academic perseverance gap" was related to the "opportunity gap." Although I am no longer employed by the district, I have been retained as independent contractor to lead this project. This positioning gave me an insider–outsider perspective.

District leadership placed constraints on the improvement process at the outset. The amount of time devoted to the improvement process was restricted to five group meetings (2 hours each) over the course of 1 year, and one-on-one meetings between site leaders (principals) and researchers during the rapid cycles of evaluation phase. Two additional (optional) group meetings were held during the rapid cycle of evaluation phase. District leadership placed these limitations because several district initiatives were already in place, and they did not want to overburden their staff.

Methodology

The study documented an improvement process in one culturally, economically, and linguistically diverse school district. The overall population is 53% Hispanic, 27% White, 14% Asian, and 6% other ethnicities. Almost half of the district's students are low income, and about one third of the students are English-as-a-second-language learners. Study participants were recruited from the three middle school site leaders (principals) who implemented rapid cycles of evaluation at their sites. All three principals participated in the study.

The study collected data through principal interviews, participant observations, and a short survey of all working group members. Two semistructured interviews were conducted with each of the three principals. The interview protocol was a condensed version of Seidman's (2013) three interview protocol because it gathers contextual information about the principals themselves and places their construction of events within that context. In addition to interviews, observations were conducted. For two of the schools, I observed a classroom where they implemented a rapid cycle of evaluation. For the third, I observed, as a participant, a meeting between the principal and assistant principal as they discussed how to get teachers to test their change idea. Additionally, a short survey was conducted to gauge working group members' opinions about the usefulness of the improvement processes, their overall experience, and their interest in continuing to learn about the processes.

Findings

The purpose of this chapter is to better understand what factors facilitate or constrain the implementation of rapid cycles of evaluation in school sites. This section discusses the unique challenges of the K–12 environment when conducting rapid cycles of evaluation. The discussion is structured around the following themes: limited teacher time for collaboration, cultural barriers, limited time among principals, and the importance of an implementation manager. Before advancing the discussion on these themes, a brief note on the implementation of the PDSA cycles is called for.

All three principals used the PDSA format of a rapid cycle of evaluation, as typically used in improvement science. They each tested one "change idea" at their site. A change idea within improvement science context denotes the strategy or intervention being tested. The change idea is usually developed through a systematic analysis of some process or practice that needs to be improved. In these examples, the change ideas were developed in collaboration with the larger district working group.

Principals A and C had a similar change idea: ask students to complete a brief reflection worksheet after exams or particular lessons. Students were asked to reflect upon their academic struggles and how they could overcome them. Additionally, Principal C tested mini-growth mindset lessons built into math classes. Principal B's change idea was repurposing library time for student goal setting. Students would set weekly goals and an adult mentor (teachers, administrators, and other staff) would provide feedback.

Within 1 to 2 weeks of initiating the rapid cycles of evaluation, it became apparent that Principal A and Principal C were struggling to get their change idea into action, whereas Principal B's implementation went smoothly. Both Principal A and C managed to get one or two teachers to try components of their ideas but had difficulty getting their teachers committed to the PDSA. In both cases, they did not follow through with the collection and study of their data. Principal B followed through in her PDSA and refined her change idea for the next PDSA cycle.

Common themes emerged for all three schools, yet there were marked differences between Principal B's experience, compared to Principal A's and Principal C's. These differences highlighted factors that facilitated and constrained the implementation of rapid cycles of evaluation in K–12 schools.

Limited Teacher Time for Collaboration

Because teachers were not included in the development of the change ideas, they did not "own" the idea. This was a limitation in the working group design. Although principals were encouraged to bring teachers to meetings, there was an obvious reluctance to do so. Unlike in health care and other fields, education poses a unique challenge when requesting teacher time for noninstructional duties.

There are contractual limits around teachers' time, including instructional time, preparation time, and time for site and district meetings. Instructional and noninstructional time is a collective bargaining right in California (and other states) and is negotiated between the teachers' union and the district (Koski & Tang, 2011). In this particular district, teachers were not required to attend more than a certain number of hours of unpaid meeting time. They could attend more with compensation, but attendance at all meetings was at the discretion of the teacher.

Thus, principals must be judicious when asking for teachers' time. In the culture of "adopt, attack, and abandon," principals are understandably skeptical of "the next big thing." During my time as district manager of research and evaluation, I encountered many principals who were disinclined to invest their own time and energy in new initiatives, let alone request teacher time, not because they did not care, but that the prevailing attitude was that "this too shall pass." Additionally, principals were aware that teachers—especially in math and English—faced more pressures than ever. In this specific district, teachers' time was already consumed with their teaching responsibilities and numerous off-site duties, such as learning Common Core and scoring local assessments. Teachers were beginning to push back. Unfortunately, the principals' desire to protect their teachers' time, as well as prevent them from becoming overwhelmed by yet another "district initiative," also prohibited them from truly collaborating with teachers on their change idea.

In Principal A's case, he proposed the two specific ideas at a math department meeting and hoped teachers would get onboard but his teachers refrained. They were skeptical of having enough class time to try the idea, and immediately wanted to make changes. Instead of making changes, Principal A became discouraged and frustrated by the unwillingness among the teachers to try something new. He did find two teachers to try the change ideas as is, but they were not invested in learning from the cycle. It appeared to be more of an exercise of compliance. They implemented pieces of the ideas but no one, including Principal A, followed through with the "study" and "act" components of the PDSA.

NEW DIRECTIONS FOR EVALUATION • DOI: 10.1002/ev

Principal C also presented the idea at a math department meeting and teachers were interested in the change idea. She communicated the idea and left it up to the teachers to execute it. Only one teacher followed through. However, the teacher and Principal C did not follow through with the "study" and "act" components of the PDSA, echoing Principal A's experience. Both principals seemed to have lost their own engagement and commitment to the PDSA as a result of the teachers losing theirs (or never having it).

Principal B was very strategic about how she chose her change idea and which teacher to approach. Her idea fit into her teacher's existing class schedule and did not require any additional teacher preparation or collaboration. This scenario proved to be crucial to her idea's successful implementation simply because it did not place any extra burden or time commitment on the teacher.

Additionally, Principal B built upon a preexisting practice at her site: Her students were already setting semester goals. She collaborated with her school implementation manager on how to test the idea of weekly goal setting. As soon as they finalized their idea, they knew exactly which teacher they wanted to recruit. They thoughtfully chose a teacher that they knew would be onboard with the idea and the PDSA.

It is improvement science's framework for studying the *process* that can break the "adopt, attack, and abandon" cycle. Principal B facilitated her PDSA process by choosing a change idea that did not require additional teacher time, and it was essential for Principals A and C to understand their process challenges in order to overcome them. Upon reflection after the attempted cycle, both Principals A and C realized the importance of early teacher collaboration when developing the change idea. Through an improvement science process map exercise conducted during one of the working group meetings, they realized the importance of getting the adults on board first. The exercise illuminated that putting an idea into action in the classroom is a process that not only requires teacher interest and commitment but also their collaboration and knowledge as to what fits and does not fit into their class time and/or lessons. By gaining this newfound knowledge, the principals learned how to improve their own implementation versus falling into the cycle of deeming the idea ineffective and abandoning it altogether.

Culture

Principal B's school was also unique in that the context of her school was an emerging "growth culture." A growth culture is similar to Peter Senge's (1990) learning organization, with less emphasis on systems learning and more on adult mindsets. In a growth culture, teachers and administrators believe they can improve their schools with continued effort, have a willingness to try new ideas, and perceive failures as a chance to learn. Principal

B considered herself a researcher by nature and promoted this culture. Her site had been going through a major redesign for the last couple years.

Principal A's and Principal C's schools had more traditional cultures. Staff were not used to change. Even minor changes could have ripple effects. Many teachers had taught there for years, and were "entrenched in the traditional." Staff were not used to collaborating with administrators. The concept of working side by side, testing an idea, failing, and learning from that failure was a deviation from their norm. Throughout the rapid cycle, Principals A and C were mindful of this entrenchment and how to best navigate it.

An incident at Principal C's school highlighted this challenge. She approached a few English teachers about participating in the PDSA to test their idea in English classes. Then, another teacher brought it up at the next English department meeting. This teacher was concerned that Principal C was not being transparent about the real reason for conducting the PDSA and asked, "Do we need to get the union?" As a result, Principal C decided not to pursue a PDSA with any English teachers, recognizing that there was a lack of trust.

Each culture influenced how the principals collaborated and communicated. As newer principals at their sites, neither Principal A nor C wanted to push too hard on their teachers. They were uncertain of how teachers would respond, and they were both aware that they needed time to build stronger relationships first. Principal A admitted that he kept the change idea "close to the vest." They hoped for volunteers at department meetings, versus seeking out specific teachers. Principal B, on the other hand, had a very specific teacher in mind, engaged her whole team in the effort, and went into the library with her teacher to implement the idea.

The entrenched traditional school culture perpetuates the "adopt, attack, abandon" mindset that prevents sustainable change. The teacher skepticism, inexperience of teachers and administrators working side by side, and reluctance of principals to push teachers too hard can all result in attacking or abandoning ideas before they are fully implemented. Teachers and principals who are interested in testing ideas may have difficulty because they do not have Deming's (1994) profound knowledge, including an understanding of resistance and the processes for testing ideas and learning from failures. They can be told to "try harder," but frustration can result when the desire is there but the knowledge or framework for how to improve is not. PDSAs provide that framework not only for adapting strategies that initially fail but also for creating a culture of collaboration and learning from failures and successes.

Lack of Principal Time

The number one barrier in schools is lack of time. Although other fields face this challenge too, the unique setting of a school renders principals in a more tentative condition when leading PDSAs. School leadership requires a constant focus and energy to keep order on their campuses. Time and energy are scarce in schools. Principals can be so busy attending to the day-to-day priorities that it is difficult to find the time to devote to other priorities, like initiatives to improve their schools. Principal A articulated his frustration with this situation: "The most challenging day at this site is wanting to do something spectacular and being stuck in the mundane."

Although principals may start with the best intentions to lead a rapid cycle of evaluation, it is easy for them to get pulled off track with "putting out fires" and the day-to-day running of their school. All three principals noted that it was hard to find the time to focus on their PDSA. As a principal, in addition to ensuring that their schools ran smoothly, they needed to switch their focus back and forth between managing their school and the bigger district initiatives. Principal A explained how they tried to manage all of this:

> For instance, we got this thing started. Then we had our accountability [session] ...We had to be ready for that. ...And then right after that, we had evaluations, too. ...Let's set our priorities. Got to work on [accountability session] then evaluations, we're piloting. So, okay, now it's four...And so, then it's almost like, "Okay, now we got...hey, wait a minute. We've got a working group [meeting], so let's get it going again." So, it's like "let's get it going again." And that's why it's been tough. It's just tough to have a single focus. ...You need as a principal to have multiple, laser focuses, but the trouble is sometimes, it just gets all blurry.

The lack of time can be especially detrimental if principals (and other potential participants) never find the time to reflect on their PDSA results—the real value comes from thinking deeply about the issue and gaining new knowledge. As noted earlier, Principals A and C recognized the importance of early teacher collaboration through a reflection on the PDSA process. Thus, helping them understand how to adapt their implementation instead of abandoning it. Principals and other working group members endorsed the power of reflection in the survey as well. When asked what they found most useful about the meetings, the most prevalent theme was the opportunity to dialogue and reflect with their colleagues.

The study results imply several strategies for easing the lack of time challenge. One is building teams through the PDSA process so that principals can delegate responsibilities. The PDSA provides a framework for parsing out roles. Another is to proactively schedule meetings for planning, follow-up, and reflection at the beginning of the PDSA rather than scheduling on an as-needed basis. Perhaps most important is the need for an implementation manager, which is further discussed in the next section.

The Importance of an Implementation Manager

Whereas Principals A and C struggled to get their idea into action, Principal B's implementation went smoothly. One of the notable differences about Principal B's experience was that she had several assistant principals who not only were willing to assist in the initiative but also were highly engaged in the effort (again, speaking to the school's culture). Most notably, she had an implementation manager, whose sole responsibility was to implement school initiatives. Principal B recognized the importance of protecting this role:

> This is just important going forward. Sometimes schools get an extra body, right? Whether it's an academic counselor, or whatever it is. And they use the resource in the wrong way. So, for example, they use it for student supervision. Or they use it for counseling of the kids, and we just made a pact from the very beginning. I'm in a pact with myself and I told the other assistant principals, [implementation manager's] role is very specific and she is not to do all these external things we do. We get caught up in the craziness, and [implementation manager] is always on the outside of the craziness. She is very busy but she doesn't have to deal with angry parents, or a kid having an emotional breakdown, or whatever it is. Or supervision, even when we are completely short on supervision, we don't ask her to go out there because we don't want her to start those things. She has to stay 100% focused on what she does.

Additionally, an implementation manager helps relieve the burden that is commonly placed on the teacher. In Principal B's case, she made a conscious decision to test something that could easily fit into the teacher's schedule and could be implemented by the implementation manager. When I observed one of the goal setting sessions, it was notable that the teacher did not have any additional responsibilities other than her typical role of overseeing the students in the library.

Although districts are understandably careful with their funding, those who want to initiate change or improvement need to invest in these key positions. With time being a major barrier, having an implementation manager is crucial to actually implementing and testing new strategies.

Implications for Practice and Evaluation

As the examples showed, school culture, available time, and the presence of an implementation manager can help or hinder a principal's ability to execute a rapid cycle of evaluation in their school. These results illustrate Feuer et al. (2002) and Berliner's (2002) assertions regarding the difficulties of school reform due to local context. Although I agree that education research may still be one of the "hardest sciences of all" (Berliner, 2002), improvement science may provide a path forward for both educators and evaluators.

Principals can use the improvement science framework to shift their context and support a growth culture. The potential of improvement science is not only that it helps leaders appreciate the steps needed to implement an idea, it is that the framework itself *is* a process. It provides an opportunity for school leaders to lead their staff through a PDSA cycle, whereby they work side by side and learn from successes and failures together. The school administrators can focus on profound knowledge—the process (getting an idea into action) and teacher engagement (versus compliance)—whereas teachers can focus on developing change ideas and their students. Per the survey, principals shared that they preferred learning with concrete examples rather than abstract ideas. By focusing on the PDSA, principals have a real experience to learn, develop, and apply process knowledge.

However, using this framework is no simple endeavor, as also demonstrated by this study. District and school leaders not only need to be dedicated to the undertaking themselves but they also need to inspire that commitment in others. Carving out that safe space for collaboration and learning requires both teacher and administrator time and resources.

For evaluators, the research illustrated how difficult it is for school leaders to implement an idea, let alone replicate an isolated randomized controlled trial intervention. Trying to implement a proven intervention or practice can prove futile without a means to fit to the local context. As the research showed, even the best intended implementation can be derailed by local culture, limited teacher collaboration time, competing priorities, and no individual focused on implementation. School leaders do not have the time, energy, or focus to engage in a fruitless effort. They need a mechanism for successfully adapting evaluated practices to their schools. The PDSA, along with improvement science's system of profound knowledge, provides that mechanism.

But perhaps the most significant implication for both practitioners and evaluators was the power of rapid cycles of evaluation to illuminate those "attack" spots before the inevitable "abandon." By providing the structure of reflection during disciplined inquiry, both through the PDSA and interviews, principals identified those trouble spots and discussed strategies for overcoming those challenges before those challenges became insurmountable. In this way, there is the potential to change the prevailing idiom of "adopt, attack, abandon" to "adopt, adapt, and accomplish."

References

Berliner, D. C. (2002). Educational research: The hardest science of all. *Educational Researcher, 31*(8), 18–20.

Bryk, A. S., Gomez, L. M., & Grunow, A. (2011). Getting ideas into action: Building networked improvement communities in education. In M. T. Hallinan (Ed.),

Frontiers in sociology of education (pp. 127–162). Dordrecht, the Netherlands: Springer Netherlands. Retrieved from http://www.springerlink.com/index/10.1007/978-94-007-1576-9_7

Deming, W. E. (1994). *The new economics for industry, government, and education* (2nd ed.). Cambridge, MA: MIT Press.

Feuer, M. J., Towne, L., & Shavelson, R. J. (2002). Scientific culture and educational research. *Educational Researcher, 31*(8), 4–14.

Koski, W. S., & Tang, A. (2011, February). *Teacher employment and collective bargaining laws in California: Structuring school district discretion over teacher employment.* Stanford, CA: Institute for Research on Education Policy and Practice. Retrieved from http://www.edpolicyinca.org/publications/teacher-employment-and-collective-bargaining-laws-california-structuring-school

Langley, G. J., Moen, R. D., Nolan, K. M., Nolan, T. W., Norman C. L., & Provost, L. P. (2009). *The improvement guide: A practical approach to enhancing organizational performance* (2nd ed.). San Francisco, CA: Jossey-Bass.

Park, S., & Takahashi, S. (2013). *90-day cycle handbook.* Stanford, CA: Carnegie Foundation for the Advancement of Teaching. Retrieved from https://carnegiefoundation.org/wp-content/uploads/2014/09/90DC_Handbook_external_10_8.pdf

Seidman, I. (2013). *Interviewing as qualitative research* (4th ed.). New York, NY: Teachers College Press.

Senge, P. M. (1990). *The fifth discipline: The art and practice of the learning organization.* New York, NY: Doubleday/Currency.

Kristen Rohanna is a doctoral student in the Social Research Methods Division at the University of California, Los Angeles.

Stigler, J. W., & Givvin, K. B. (2017). Online learning as a wind tunnel for improving teaching. In C. A. Christie, M. Inkelas & S. Lemire (Eds.), *Improvement Science in Evaluation: Methods and Uses. New Directions for Evaluation, 153*, 79–91.

6

Online Learning as a Wind Tunnel for Improving Teaching

James W. Stigler, Karen B. Givvin

Abstract

Attempts to improve teaching through research have met with limited success. This is, in part, due to the fact that teaching is a complex cultural system that has evolved over long periods of time—multiply determined and inherently resistant to change. But it is also true that research on teaching is difficult to carry out. Using traditional educational research methodologies, testing new methods of teaching requires, first, that teachers be able to implement the method at a scale sufficient for study, that random assignment of teachers to conditions can be feasibly carried out, and that ecological validity of the treatment can be preserved. In this chapter, we propose an alternative approach that combines the affordances of online learning with the methodologies of systems improvement. Using an analogy from the development of the airplane, we discuss how online learning might be a wind tunnel for the study and improvement of teaching. © 2017 Wiley Periodicals, Inc., and the American Evaluation Association.

Processes of teaching and learning lie at the very core of education. Yet, improving teaching has proven to be one of the most difficult challenges facing education researchers and reformers. In this chapter, we reflect on why something so pervasive and seemingly straightforward as teaching has been so resistant to change, and even to research. We then discuss a new approach—grounded in improvement science and supported by education technology—that we believe has great potential for improving teaching.

Improving Teaching: Why It's Hard

There is a long tradition of research on teaching. Each new generation, it seems, seeks to reinvent or reinvigorate what appears to be a straightforward approach: measure various aspects of teaching, identify those that are associated with desired student outcomes, then focus improvement efforts on those critical variables. Why is this so hard to do?

More Than the Sum of the Variables: Teaching Is System

One reason it's hard is that teaching is more than an assemblage of variables. It is a complex system in which the impact of one variable may depend on the others in complicated ways and the causal impact on learning is neither simple nor straightforward. We are led to this conclusion mainly for one reason: attempts to identify the critical variables that define teaching quality have been largely unsuccessful, as have reform efforts based on such variables.

These attempts have emerged from two different research traditions. One of these is classroom research. In this tradition, researchers have sought to describe classroom teaching by measuring variables hypothesized to affect student learning outcomes. Sometimes the variables are rooted in theories of learning, for example, behaviorism (in the 1960s and 70s) or cognitive psychology (in the 90s and today), whereas at other times, they emerge from detailed qualitative observations of classrooms. In both cases, the results have been disappointing. Nuthall (2005), for example, describes his own personal journey to crack the code of teaching and learning, a journey largely marked by disappointments, but an interesting read in any case. Through a series of studies employing a range of methodologies over a 40-year period, Nuthall failed to find anything he could measure about teaching that was significantly correlated with student learning outcomes. A more recent attempt is the large Gates Foundation-funded project, Measures of Effective Teaching. In this study, which is perhaps the largest and most highly funded study ever conducted, only a few small correlations were found (Kane & Staiger, 2012).

Another research tradition starts not with observations in classrooms but with theories developed in the laboratory. These researchers tend to come from the cognitive and learning sciences, and they have produced some fascinating results—in the lab. For example, Bjork and colleagues have shown that spacing and interleaving of items to be studied produces greater learning than does blocking of items (i.e., grouping items of a type together), even though learners themselves do not perceive this to be the case (Bjork & Bjork, 2011; Kornell & Bjork, 2008). As robust as these effects are in laboratory studies, they have rarely been effectively transferred into the classroom, mainly because there is a lot more going on in a classroom than can be captured by a single variable.

Regardless of where the variables come from—whether from learning theory or empirical observation—it is not easy to create an effective lesson out of a list of variables, even if those variables have been shown to be effective "all other things being equal." Teaching and learning make up a complex system of interacting parts, and it is very hard to change one part without affecting the others. At a macro level of analysis, the system of classroom teaching and learning includes the teacher, the students, curriculum content, teaching routines, materials, district and state policies, assessments, physical layout of the classroom, parents, homework, and so on. Even in the best-case scenario, no single variable is likely to have a large effect on student outcome.

Teaching Is a Cultural Activity

So yes, teaching is a system, and a complex system. But that's not all. It is a cultural system—a set of routines, supported by widely held beliefs and values, that have evolved over long periods of time and that represent a hard-fought compromise between the desired and the possible. Why do we think that teaching is a cultural activity? We aren't the first to make this assertion (e.g., Gallimore, 1996). But we found the idea a compelling one as we worked through our analyses of data from the Trends in International Mathematics and Science Study (TIMSS) video studies (Stigler & Hiebert, 1998, 1999/2009).

In these studies, national probability samples of videos of classroom instruction—eighth-grade mathematics and science lessons, to be specific—were compared across eight different countries, some high performing and others (such as the United States) not. Like other classroom studies, we failed to find clear observational correlates of cross-national differences in mathematics and science achievement. But more important for our purposes here, we found large discrepancies in teaching routines across, but not within, countries, even among the high-achieving countries (Givvin, Hiebert, Jacobs, Hollingsworth, & Gallimore, 2005). Thus, to a greater extent than we would have predicted, teaching routines within a country—even one as diverse as the United States—appear to vary little when viewed from a cross-national perspective.

Cultural activities are learned implicitly, through participation from an early age. Even though we might wish that teachers would learn how to teach from teacher education programs, the evidence suggests that teachers largely just teach the way they, themselves, were taught. Cultural activities are hard to see. Because the routines are widely shared within a culture, we tend not to notice aspects, even those that may prove critical for student learning. And cultural activities are hard to change. They are hard to

New Directions for Evaluation • DOI: 10.1002/ev

change, first, because they tend to lie outside our awareness. Cultural activities are also hard to change because they are multiply determined. We may try to change some aspect of our teaching. But when we do, we almost certainly will get pushback from the rest of the system: students will complain, parents will question the change, textbooks become difficult to use because they are not aligned with the change, and so on. The difficulty of putting the Common Core standards into place in classrooms and the often vitriolic opposition to them is just one example of pushback from the larger system.

The cultural nature of teaching presents a methodological challenge to researchers seeking to understand the relationship of teaching to learning. In order to conduct an experimental test of a new teaching method, we first must get a sufficient number of teachers to adopt the change and be able to implement it faithfully in their classrooms. Education is a human-made institution, which means we are free to innovate and create something fundamentally different from what existed before—*in theory*. On the other hand, we don't see a lot of natural variation in teaching within a culture, and you cannot study what you cannot implement on a large enough scale (Gallimore & Santagata, 2006). Changing teaching is notoriously hard, even for research purposes.

Why Labs Settings and Randomized Controlled Trials Aren't the Answer

As articulated in this chapter, laboratory models have their limitations. Even though they may help us to avoid the tricky challenges inherent in changing teaching, they suffer from a lack of ecological validity, which is heightened by the fact that teaching is a complex system. Laboratory models, typically focused on one or a small number of variables, yield interesting theoretical results but are unlikely to transfer easily to the complex system of teaching in schools.

But these are not the only challenges to our traditional research methodologies. The "gold standard" of education research—the randomized controlled trial (RCT)—has some serious limitations, even when the challenges of implementation have been met. The studies are expensive, largely because of the challenges already outlined. Furthermore, even though reaching a statistical criterion of $p < .05$ may qualify a study as publishable, it is still true that it is a measure of average effects. Much of the variance is left unexplained and most researchers who conduct RCTs do little to learn from the variability within conditions, even though the intervention being studied may be helpful for some students and harmful to others. And, the interventions studied tend not to be interpretable in the context of theory—what Lipsey (1993) refers to as "small theories"—which makes them very difficult to adapt to new students and contexts. There must be a better way.

Improving Systems

We have argued thus far that teaching is a complex cultural system and also that the nature of teaching presents methodological challenges to those wishing to study and improve it. But there is another research tradition—one we will call improvement science—that has developed explicitly for the purpose of improving complex systems. In this section, we discuss this tradition and assess its applicability to the problem of improving teaching.

Roots of Improvement Science

The pioneers of improvement science—Deming, Shewhart, Juran, and others—developed their methodologies largely in industrial and manufacturing contexts. Recently, however, great strides have been made in applying the principles of improvement science to health care and some impressive results have been achieved (Gawande, 2007, 2010; Kenney, 2008). Educators often resent the analogy of education and manufacturing, but then, healthcare professionals have voiced similar objections. Although we don't want to gloss over the differences, we do want to explore the methodologies, especially because they have led to some impressive accomplishments in the medical world.

Deming posited four pillars of improvement science: appreciation of a system, understanding variation, human psychology, and the theory of knowledge development. Systems thinking is perhaps the most important. Deming observed that we often fail to see the system that produces the outcomes we are interested in; instead, we tend to zero in on a single variable. In manufacturing, for example, variations in quality result from a number of factors, including random ones. Yet, we mistakenly (in Deming's view) blame the worker for low-quality products, failing to see the system that led to the result. Paul Batalden, one of the pioneers of improvement science in health care, reportedly said: "Every system is perfectly designed to achieve the results that it gets." The first step in improving a system is to see and understand the system the way it works now.

Whereas traditional education researchers are typically satisfied when the variance between an intervention and a control group is greater than that within, the improvement scientist seeks to understand and reduce variation to within acceptable limits. If a system produces great variation—as is true of educational outcomes in general—it is not enough just to know that the average of one group is greater than another. It is important to understand the root of the variation and then make improvements in the process to both reduce variation (i.e., by bringing up the low achievers to acceptable levels) and improve the level of outcomes overall. Improvement scientists have developed statistical techniques for analyzing variability that are specifically designed to help understand and improve the outcomes of complex systems. As discussed by Berwick (2015) in a recent talk, R. A. Fisher developed statistics that target improvement of simple systems;

New Directions for Evaluation • DOI: 10.1002/ev

Walter Shewhart developed the statistical techniques that are the foundation for modern improvement science.

Psychology is important, of course, because human actors are part of many of the complex systems we care about most and that are most difficult to improve. If a better method of teaching is discovered that does not mean, it will be adopted in schools. Teachers would need to believe it is better for their students and that it is feasible to implement the method in the contexts in which they work. Psychology is also important for reasons that go beyond the role envisioned by Deming. Theories of psychology are a primary source of hypotheses to guide the development of new ideas for teaching and learning.

Finally, the tradition of improvement science specifies a disciplined methodology for iterative improvement and knowledge development, a methodology that includes the idea of Plan–Do–Study–Act (PDSA) cycles. This theory of knowledge development has been described in a variety of ways, but all can be encompassed in a common framework called the Model for Improvement (Langley, 2009).[1] It includes two components, the first of which is a series of three questions that guide the work:

1. What specifically are we trying to accomplish?
2. What change might we introduce, and why?
3. How will we know that a change is actually an improvement?

Answering these questions involves some important and often difficult pieces of work. Questions one and three go together, three being the question of measurement. As Bryk, Gomez, Grunow, and LeMahieu (2015) point out, "We cannot improve at scale what we cannot measure" (p.111). Langley et al. (2009) propose that we need at least three kinds of measures to do the work of improvement: measures of outcomes, measures of process, and balancing measures (to make sure that a change to improve one outcome does not accidentally make some other valued outcome worse).

Measures of process are important because they help to validate the theory behind a change. Theories are important because only if you *understand* the system will you be able to both reduce variation to within acceptable limits and successfully adapt improvements to new settings. Thus, it is important not only to develop a change idea but also to have some idea of why you expect the change idea to result in an improvement.

The second component of the improvement framework is the iterative methodology for testing changes, the PDSA cycle. PDSA cycles are small tests of change that use the scientific method (see Figure 6.1).[2] Importantly, PDSA cycles are conducted on an appropriate scale and in the

---

[1] This model has been introduced into education most prominently by Bryk et al. (2015).
[2] Much has been written elsewhere about the PDSA cycle. See Langley et al. (2009) and Rother (2009) for two alternative yet complementary formulations.

Figure 6.1. Overview of the PDSA Cycle

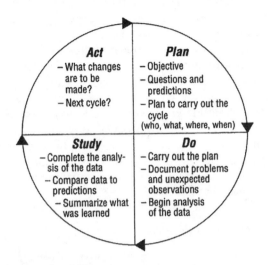

Source: Langley, Nolan, & Nolan, 1994

actual site where the system operates (Langley et al., 2009; Moen & Norman, 2006). Thus, from the very beginning, changes in the system that succeed have some ecological validity. If the costs of failure are high, or readiness for change is low, it's wise to start with very small-scale tests. Later, as the knowledge base grows, it will be possible to scale up to more sites (Parry, 2014; Rossi, 1987). The goal is to avoid going out in a Hail Mary flame of defeat based only on minimal evidence.

Each PDSA cycle is typically carried out over a brief period—the smallest test possible to enable the team to learn from the work. Cycles end with a decision to adopt, adapt, or abandon the change. Usually, the decision is to adapt; enough is learned to suggest how further modifications might lead to better outcomes with lower variation.

Applications to Teaching

The improvement methodology described here has been successfully used in education, though not widely. The most famous example is Japanese lesson study (Lewis, 2000, 2015; Stigler & Hiebert, 1999/2009). In lesson study, the unit chosen as the focus of the improvement work is a single classroom lesson. The lesson is chosen, we surmise, because it is the smallest authentic unit that includes all relevant aspects of the system of teaching that is to be improved. Thus, it has ecological validity, ensuring that the changes developed and the generalizable mechanisms discovered in the context of a single lesson might be applicable to other sites and to other lessons.

NEW DIRECTIONS FOR EVALUATION • DOI: 10.1002/ev

But lesson study is difficult to implement. In the United States, the culture of teaching and the organization of the teacher's work week make it difficult for teachers to work together on improving teaching. The lack of a national curriculum (which they have in Japan) means that the work done at one site may be less applicable to other sites, reducing the efficiencies of the improvement process. And even in Japan, lessons only partly meet the requirement of being a repeatable process—something fundamental to the assumptions of improvement science. If something cannot be repeated continuously, it is difficult to engage in the repeated tests (i.e., PDSA cycles) needed to yield results over time. It is true that teachers teach lessons every day. But the content of the lessons changes over the course of a year. So although it is possible to test more general aspects of pedagogy, there are limitations on what can be tested in an iterative fashion, at least in the short term, by a single teacher.

Online Learning as a Wind Tunnel

Much has been written about the development of the airplane (e.g., Baals & Corliss, 1981; Bradshaw, 2005; McCullough, 2015). Without getting into the controversies of interest to historians, it is interesting to note that at least some historians see the development of the wind tunnel as a critical event in aviation history. Prior to the advent of the wind tunnel, which was invented at the end of the 19th century, aviators would build flying machines and then launch them, usually with themselves attached. The cost of failure was high: each time a plane crashed it would take a long time to rebuild it, not to mention the effect failure had on test pilots. One could describe these trials and errors as a sequence of PDSA cycles. But it was a slow process. With a wind tunnel, a model plane could be built, tested, and modified within a relatively short period of time and with a substantial reduction in risk and expense. Advances after the wind tunnel were rapid.

We propose that online learning provides a wind tunnel for the improvement of teaching. If classroom teaching is implemented face to face, one teacher with many students, teaching a particular curriculum, it is hard to make iterative changes and test them with students. If one is testing a change in a particular lesson, which is part of a particular unit, it generally isn't possible to test a new change until the next time that lesson comes along, which might be a semester or even a year later.

Online education, on the other hand, presents us with new opportunities for research and improvement. Teachers participating in the improvement project can collectively design online lessons (e.g., videos with interactive prompts) and study students' learning outcomes. Based on what they find, they can design changes, incorporate them into the lesson material, and provide the revised lesson to a new group of students, immediately. Individual students can be randomly assigned to get different instruction, and thus teachers can study variation both within and across groups, on a continuous basis. And, because online lessons can be accessed from anywhere at any time, the number of students who could be included in improvement research could, conceivably, be quite large. Like an airplane in a wind tunnel, iterative testing of instructional methods and materials can be conducted rapidly. We don't deny that the fine-tuning of the lessons will need to take place in live classrooms, but much of the work can be completed online. What the wind tunnel provides is a mechanism for implementing more rapid PDSA cycles—more rapid than can be implemented in regular classrooms, alone—enhancing and augmenting the improvement process.

Improvement methodologies are easily applied to online teaching. The Model for Improvement, PDSA cycles, and the statistical techniques of improvement science, discussed previously, might all be brought to bear on the study of online teaching. And if all we learn is how to make better online courses, that would be a worthwhile pursuit. In contrast with aviation, in the case of online learning, the wind tunnel is itself a meaningful end point. All that is learned there can be directly applied to the explosion of online instructional resources. But as a wind tunnel, online learning can also provide us with a laboratory model to use for understanding and improving the more general processes of teaching and learning, whether they be implemented in a live classroom or in a virtual environment. An example of how this might work comes from a recent project we have been developing in our lab.

Example: Learning from Instructional Conversations

An important goal of education is understanding: We want our students not only to learn the facts and procedures of a domain but we also want them to understand the core concepts that underlie the procedures and organize the domain. Research comparing novices with experts reveals that experts see problems differently than novices. Chi, Glaser, and Rees (1982), in a classic study, found that novices tend to classify physics problems based on their surface features (e.g., "rotational things," "pulleys and weights," or "objects on an inclined plane"), whereas expert physicists classify problems according to the physics principles at work (e.g., "conservation of energy law" or "Newton's Second Law"). Connecting concepts to problems makes the experts' knowledge more flexible and powerful in novel problem situations.

Producing students who understand turns out to be highly challenging. We know from extensive research in cognitive psychology that practices such as self-explanation that engage learners in actively connecting problems and procedures to concepts do promote learning with understanding. But we also know that attempts to create these kinds of practices in classrooms have proven extremely difficult. Gallimore and colleagues (Tharp & Gallimore, 1991), for example, identified a classroom discourse pattern they called the "instructional conversation." They also found that through intensive work with teachers, they could create this kind of discourse pattern from scratch. But they failed, in the end, to find a way to implement instructional conversations at scale (an obstacle discussed also by Rossi, 1987). The cultural nature of teaching makes it nearly impossible to change something as deeply internalized as the routines of talk that define teacher–student interactions.

The fact that instructional conversations cannot be created at scale is problematic in two ways. First, if we cannot create instructional conversations in a large number of classrooms, it will be very difficult to research how such discourse patterns affect students' processing of, and learning from, classroom instruction (Gallimore & Santagata, 2006). Second, even if we assume that such instructional forms are highly effective for producing deep understanding, unless we can create such instructional conditions at scale we still will not be able to produce the kind of learning we desire. Which leads us to ask: Can we, by using online learning technologies, build a model of the instructional conversation (similar to the model airplane that one might build) and a wind tunnel in which to test it?

This has been a focus of recent work in our lab. First, we are attempting to study how students learn from instructional conversations by simulating their participation in such conversations online. Our first step in this work is to create and implement classroom lessons that exemplify the kind of instructional conversations we are interested in studying. In one project, carried out by Belinda Thompson, we created a series of lessons on algebraic expressions and equations. These lessons were designed for community college students taking a beginning algebra class—a developmental mathematics course designed to prepare students for college-level mathematics. The lessons were taught by an expert teacher to a group of community college students and videotaped. The teacher engaged students in a series of rich instructional conversations that focused on core concepts of beginning algebra.

The videos of the class were next uploaded to the cloud and then turned into online instructional modules by embedding interactive prompts and questions into the video. By having a different group of students engage with the online modules, we thus have created a simulation model that creates at least a semblance of what the experience of engaging in an instructional conversation might be like. No, it is not a perfect model, just as a tiny airplane placed in a wind tunnel would not have room for passengers! But it is an experience that can be more easily studied than a live classroom experience.

We are just beginning our studies using these videos. In the studies, we can have students study the videos as if they were participants in the live class. We can, using interactive software, have the video stop, for example, just as a student in the class makes a comment. And then we can have the student watching the video respond with the comment they would make were they in the class. Students can be randomly assigned to watch different video clips and to respond to different prompts and questions in the same video. For example, we might ask one group of students to solve a problem posed in the video, another to explain its solution to a hypothetical student, and a third to represent the solution graphically. In this way, we (i.e., our small team of researchers and community college instructors) can rapidly develop and test hypotheses about the factors that govern students' thinking as they process the contents of a rich mathematical discussion and we can adapt lessons to reflect what we learn. Applying the techniques of improvement science, we can, over time, optimize students' learning from such instructional conversations. The results of this work can be applied in two settings: first, to the development of better online learning experiences that can more easily be deployed at scale; second, to the design of better curricula to guide live classroom discussion.

Concluding Thoughts

The methods of improvement science have great potential for improving teaching and learning. But realizing that potential has been difficult, in part, because of the nature of education systems. Settings in which a single teacher works with the same group of students over an extended period of time are not easily subjected to improvement methodologies, which require, above all, that there be a repeatable process that can be iteratively studied and improved. Simply put, the U.S. school system, as it currently exists, makes it difficult for improvement science to scale and spread as an internalized learning system. Online learning, to a large extent, offers a partial solution to this problem, making it possible to define repeatable instructional routines that are subject to experimental control. Teachers, the process owners, can be as involved in the study of online teaching as they would have been the study of their own classroom lessons. Because they will still need to adapt the online lessons to work in the context of their classrooms, online learning isn't a final solution, but because online learning can be used to more efficiently identify and test possible improvements that can be adapted to individual classrooms, it seems to us a very good start.

In this sense, online learning, finally, provides us with a wind tunnel that, though it cannot teach us everything we need to know, can provide us a way to advance knowledge and optimize learning without the risks of crashing. Its use is scalable, with at least some degree of ecological validity, and it offers opportunities for random assignment without sacrificing consistency in implementation. When combined with the processes of improvement science, online instructional modules can support the study of the complex system that is teaching. We are only just beginning to understand the potential of this work.

It is important to note that this kind of research and improvement cannot be done by researchers alone. It is true that researchers are a fertile source of change ideas, mainly because they can bring theories to bear on understanding the mechanisms that produce learning. But as John Dewey (1929) pointed out long ago, research itself—especially research carried out in laboratories—will never produce ready-made rules to guide the improvement of teaching. Research, Dewey said, can make us sensitive to the factors that interact to produce learning. But simple rules will never be enough to tame the complexities of a system as complex as education.

References

Baals, D. D., & Corliss, W. R. (1981). *Wind tunnels of NASA*. Washington, DC: National Aeronautics and Space Administration.

Berwick, D. (2015). *Keynote address*. Carnegie Foundation Summit on Improving Education, San Francisco, CA.

Bjork, E. L., & Bjork, R. A. (2011). Making things hard on yourself, but in a good way: Creating desirable difficulties to enhance learning. In M. A. Gernsbacher (Ed.), *Psychology and the real world: Essays illustrating fundamental contributions to society* (pp. 56–64). New York, NY: Worth Publishers.

Bradshaw, G. (2005). What's so hard about rocket science? Secrets the rocket boys knew. In M. Gorman, R. Tweney, D. Gooding, & A. Kincannon (Eds.), *Scientific and technological thinking* (pp. 259–275). Hillsdale, NJ: Erlbaum.

Bryk, A. S., Gomez, L. M., Grunow, A., & LeMahieu, P. G. (2015). *Learning to improve: How America's schools can get better at getting better*. Cambridge, MA: Harvard Education Press.

Chi, M. T. H., Glaser, R., & Rees, E. (1982). Expertise in problem solving. In R. Sternberg (Ed.), *Advances in the psychology of human intelligence* (Vol. 1, pp. 7–76). Hillsdale, NJ: Erlbaum.

Dewey, J. (1929). *The sources of a science of education*. New York, NY: Liveright.

Gallimore, R. (1996). Classrooms are just another cultural activity. In B. K. Keogh & D. L. Speece (Eds.), *Research on classroom ecologies: Implications for inclusion of children with learning disabilities* (pp. 229–250). Mahwah, NJ: Lawrence Erlbaum Associates.

Gallimore, R., & Santagata, R. (2006). Researching teaching: The problem of studying a system resistant to change. In R. R. Bootzin & P. E. McKnight (Eds.), *Strengthening research methodology: Psychological measurement and evaluation* (pp. 11–28). Washington, DC: APA Books.

Gawande, A. (2007). *Better: A surgeon's notes on performance*. New York, NY: Metropolitan.

Gawande, A. (2010). *The checklist manifesto: How to get things right*. New York, NY: Metropolitan Books.

Givvin, K. B., Hiebert, J., Jacobs, J. K., Hollingsworth, H., & Gallimore, R. (2005). Are there national patterns of teaching? Evidence from the TIMSS 1999 video study. *Comparative Education Review, 49*(3), 311–343.

Kane, T. J., & Staiger, D. O. (2012). *Gathering feedback for teaching: Combining high-quality observations with student surveys and achievement gains. Research paper*. MET Project. Seattle, WA: Bill & Melinda Gates Foundation.

Kenney, C. (2008). *The best practice: How the new quality movement is transforming medicine*. New York, NY: Public Affairs.

Kornell, N., & Bjork, R. A. (2008). Learning concepts and categories: Is spacing the "enemy of induction"? *Psychological Science, 19*, 585–592.

Langley, G. J., Moen, R., Nolan, K. M., Nolan, T. W., Norman, C. L., & Provost, L. P. (2009). *The improvement guide: A practical approach to enhancing organizational performance*. San Francisco, CA: Jossey-Bass.

Langley, G. J., Nolan, K. M., & Nolan, T. W. (1994). The foundation of improvement. *Quality Progress, 27*(6), 81–86.

Lewis, C. (2000). *Lesson study: The core of Japanese professional development.* Paper presented at the Annual Meeting of the American Educational Research Association, New Orleans, LA.

Lewis, C. (2015). What is improvement science? Do we need it in education? *Educational Researcher, 44*(1), 54–61.

Lipsey, M. W. (1993). Theory as method: Small theories of treatments. In L. B. Sechrest & A. G. Scott (Eds.), *New Directions for Program Evaluation: No. 57. Understanding causes and generalizing about them* (pp. 5–38). San Francisco, CA: Jossey-Bass.

McCullough, D. (2015). *The Wright brothers.* New York, NY: Simon & Schuster.

Moen, R., & Norman, C. (2006). *Evolution of the PDCA cycle.* Retrieved from http://pkpinc.com/files/NA01MoenNormanFullpaper.pdf

Nuthall, G. (2005). The cultural myths and realities of classroom teaching and learning: A personal journey. *Teachers College Record, 107*(5), 895–934.

Parry, G. J. (2014). A brief history of quality improvement. *Journal of Oncology Practice, 10*(3), 196–199.

Rossi, P. (1987). The iron law of evaluation and other metallic rules. *Research in Social Problems and Public Policy, 4*, 3–20.

Rother, M. (2009). *Toyota kata: Managing people for improvement, adaptiveness and superior results.* San Francisco, CA: McGraw-Hill Professional.

Stigler, J. W., & Hiebert, J. (1998). Teaching is a cultural activity. *American Educator, 22*(4), 4–11.

Stigler, J. W., & Hiebert, J. (1999/2009). *The teaching gap: Best ideas from the world's teachers for improving education in the classroom.* New York, NY: Simon and Schuster.

Tharp, R. G., & Gallimore, R. (1991). *Rousing minds to life: Teaching, learning, and schooling in social context.* New York, NY: Cambridge University Press.

JAMES W. STIGLER is professor of psychology at the University of California, Los Angeles, director of the TIMSS video studies, and founder of LessonLab Inc.

KAREN B. GIVVIN is a researcher and adjunct professor at UCLA, in the Department of Psychology. Her research focuses on better understanding students' mathematical knowledge—especially their misunderstandings—and how teachers might use that information to improve instruction.

Inkelas, M., Christie, C. A., & Lemire, S. (2017). Value and opportunity for improvement science in evaluation. In C. A. Christie, M. Inkelas & S. Lemire (Eds.), *Improvement Science in Evaluation: Methods and Uses. New Directions for Evaluation, 153*, 93–102.

7

Value and Opportunity for Improvement Science in Evaluation

Moira Inkelas, Christina A. Christie, Sebastian Lemire

This chapter focuses on features of improvement science that the evaluation field could benefit from, drawing from case examples. Themes addressed include learning from error, learning from and reducing variation, systems thinking, and learning for scale. We also consider opportunities for professional development, whereby evaluation professionals and people in practice can successfully apply improvement science techniques and methods within and across fields and in the complex systems that shape health, social, and educational outcomes. Finally, we describe resource and management challenges of building improvement science into the evaluation repertoire. © 2017 Wiley Periodicals, Inc., and the American Evaluation Association.

Value and Opportunity for Improvement Science in Evaluation

This volume illustrates how fields such as education and health care can apply improvement science to solve problems in systems. Improvement science uses evaluative methods to support progressive cycles of learning and action with the goal of optimizing a process or system. Based on a production mindset, this approach intends to improve the degree of belief that a change will lead to an improvement, in a specified context, using iterative learning cycles to adopt, amend, or abandon concepts and strategies (Deming, 2000; Langley et al., 2009). Improvement science enables users to customize a new process or intervention to work under the range of conditions that exist within a system, make them scale ready so that implementers can put them into place in real-world settings, make them reliable (producing consistent results), and sustain them (Moen, 2002; Scoville, Little, Rakover, Luther, & Mate, 2016).

As stated in the introduction, the purpose of the present volume is to promote ideas, techniques, and tools between evaluation and improvement science. Evaluators are concerned with use (the extent to which evaluation practice promotes use of its findings), valuing (how judgments about programs are determined in evaluation), and methods (the extent of methodological rigor and knowledge generation). Chapter 2 shows how improvement science contrasts with, and potentially augments, common evaluation practice by offering strategies to learn from error; learn from variation and reduce unwanted variation; use systems thinking to understand how context affects cause-and-effect relationships; and create scale-ready interventions. Chapters 3–6 offer examples of improvement science that address the questions of use, valuing, and methods. This chapter considers the implications of hallmark strategies of improvement science for evaluators.

Learning from Error

Although both evaluation and improvement science share an interest in using results to support or reject prevailing theories about cause and effect, improvement science is primarily concerned with use of deductive and inductive learning that refines theory so that practitioners can predict how a strategy will work into the future (Moen, Nolan, & Provost, 2012). All learning cycles lead to an explicit action, in small tests of one as well as in larger-scale tests such as prototypes or pilots (Moen, 2002). The chapters in this volume offer examples of coupling the deductive portion of "plan" and "do" based on existing theory with the inductive portion of "study" and "act." Frequently, change that did not work as predicted leads to refinement of the theory. This represents a shift in both mindset and approach for evaluation practitioners who typically design studies to test a theory that is believed to work, rather than to combine information about what has and has not worked as an optimization process.

Improvement science offers a method of learning from error that minimizes the adverse consequences of what might otherwise be viewed as failure. One way is by experimenting at the scale that is appropriate for the degree of belief about a change. Specifically, Brown, Kahn, and Goyal (Chapter 3) and Rohanna (Chapter 5) show how to reduce the consequences of error by matching the scale of a test with the degree of belief that the change will result in an improvement. These examples use small-scale testing and real-time measures displayed in time series format to detect the immediate impact of changes. Reducing the negative consequences of a result that does not match the theory may increase willingness to introduce ideas that are promising but may not work in their current form. This makes it easier to test a wider set of innovative solutions to social problems. Brown, Kahn, and Goyal (Chapter 3) illustrate this approach in health care; Inkelas, Bowie and Guirguis (Chapter 4) illustrate it in a cross-sector change initiative; and Rohanna (Chapter 5) illustrates it in education.

Evaluators also learn from error, but the focus on outcomes, combined with a tendency to implement and study at a large scale, have in many ways served to depress the room for error and any learning that might ensue from this. The stepwise experimentation central to improvement science offers a way of reducing the adverse consequences of discovering that a hypothesized improvement did not lead to the intended result. This creates a space for progressive learning that is especially valuable in studying interventions in complex systems, where impact of a change is not as easy to predict and where adaptation is the expectation, not the exception.

Learning from Variation

Examining variation—and identifying implementation-outcome patterns—offers insight into why and how one or more factors of interest lead to a result. As evaluators know well, it is the "why" and "how" questions, the identification of critical program ingredients, that generate knowledge of how to successfully implement changes across settings and in systems. Inkelas, Bowie, and Guirguis (Chapter 4) offer a community systems example of examining variation in care processes across organizations and sectors to spark questions about the reasons for it. These insights help organizations to consider what they could modify to get the results of better-performing peers. Visualizing data in time series enables an organization or system to reduce unwanted variation in a process, which may be due to differences in execution or the insight that a particular setting or population subgroup may require a modified process, among other things.

In improvement science, there is no assumption that context does not affect implementation. Rather, what is critical is that contextual information is integrated into the learning process to better understand how programs can be adapted to work in the various contexts of real-world practice, so that they can eventually be implemented at scale with consistent results across settings. Progressive testing of changes enables us to learn how they work under different conditions. This may lead to standardization in which the same process is practiced or where processes are modified and then standardized for a range of implementation contexts. Brown, Kahn, and Goyal (Chapter 3) show the importance of understanding practice-level variation in workflows to determine which member of a care team should carry out a new process that has been shown to be effective. Likewise, Rohanna (Chapter 5) describes a similar context-responsive improvement process within a school, effectively translating a "one-size-fits-all" school reform to work within local school contexts through a sequence of rapid learning cycles (i.e., Plan–Do–Study–Act [PDSA] cycles). Contextual constraints such as limited teacher time and local school culture informed the iterative cycles of adaptation. The resulting strategies have a greater chance of leading to desired results for different teachers and schools.

A practical implication for evaluators of learning from variation is the importance of those closest to the process being involved in generating and testing ideas. Learning from variation requires close attention to context, and this is why improvement science relies on stakeholders being invested in the change process and on data that is disaggregated to the level of the stakeholder. Rohanna (Chapter 5) describes local actors' investment in the school reform change process, whereby barriers related to principal and teacher time as well as different school cultures were diminished.

Evaluators also acknowledge variation; the growing body of books, articles, and conference presentations speaks to a sustained interest in this important topic. But we often attempt to control for contextual variation with randomization or use contextual factors as variables in a model, often without fully explaining their hypothesized effect. Many of our designs and analytical strategies aim to "control for," "rule out," or "hold constant" the influence of context. This all-too-common view of context as "noise" to be silenced is unfortunate. Many evaluations simply fail to examine how and why cause and effect varies with context. From this perspective, the use of rapid PDSA cycles, as just one example, represents a highly relevant and useful approach in many evaluative contexts.

Systems Thinking

Evaluators have a growing appreciation that interventions operate within systems. Systems thinking recognizes the dynamic interdependence of factors. It places the focus on the system as a whole, rather than its component parts (Meadows, 2008). Systems thinking focuses on the outcome and how the interdependent parts influence it (Gharajedaghi, 2011). Although evaluators commonly use analytic thinking that examines the contribution of multiple independent variables, the field is increasingly grappling with the implications of systems thinking in which variables are understood to be interdependent and often dynamic, not static. Systems thinking provides a framework for understanding of the complex interplay of people, policies, and practices in any community or organization in which we might want to introduce change. Evaluators are searching for ways to incorporate these concepts into evaluation practice, ways in which to bridge the conceptual and the practical.

The chapters in the present volume offer examples of systems thinking within improvement science. Inkelas, Bowie, and Guirguis (Chapter 4) describe the use of improvement science to support a shared change process across multiple autonomous, interdependent organizations that serve families in a geographic community. Recognizing the need for organized data-driven learning and action over time, rather than for a single intervention or set of interventions, the initiative offers a prototype of a community system of facilitative leadership focused on shared outcomes and process improvement methods.

Learning for Scale

With its roots in production, improvement science intends to produce changes that work at the scale of a system. This is often the "Achilles heel" of intervention development; that is, developing changes that work and sustain when implemented across school districts, health systems, community systems, and so on. The challenge of scaling interventions to achieve desired outcomes has not been lost on evaluators (see Weiss, 2010). However, guidance on how to scale up interventions is limited. The failure may be an execution problem (not implementing the intervention as specified), a learning problem (not testing the intervention under all of the operational conditions before implementing at scale), or both. Improvement science offers a strategy for learning enough about an intervention, including its underlying theory and its mechanisms, to increase the chances of success when implemented at scale (Moen, 2002).

Several chapters in this volume show learning processes geared toward discovering what will work at the desired scale. Similar to formative evaluation, improvement science uses iterative progressive learning that continues until a process is nearly perfected at the scale at which it is expected to perform. This is the goal of improvement science and has been the basis of effective scale-up in organizations, systems, and even countries (Langley et al., 2009; Massoud et al., 2006). For example, a common strategy is to try to solve a problem completely for one person and then apply those solutions for several more people to learn if breakdowns occur. At each level of scale, from 1 to 5 to 25 people and so on, the improvement team either solves the system barrier that emerges or reworks the idea so that it can work at the next level of scale. For example, if the change fails to work at the level of 25 people, it may be necessary to identify another stakeholder in the system who has the requisite time or skill to manage a process. At each level of scale, the question is if and how the idea should be done in a different way to fit within the system. Brown, Kahn, and Goyal (Chapter 3) describe such a strategy for developing healthcare innovations. Evaluators also use qualitative or case study information for developing changes, but improvement science offers an iterative progression of learning. Brown, Kahn, and Goyal (Chapter 3) also illustrate how an improvement team progressively refines its working theory by adding new concepts until the system has achieved and is sustaining a sufficient level of reliability.

Another aspect of learning for scale that addresses a common practical challenge is starting in the strongest and most feasible area of the theory in the face of limited resources and bandwidth of participants. Several chapters in this volume use improvement science to test parts of the theory in a resourced environment while keeping the features of more highly challenged environments in mind. Resource constraints with respect to innovation and improvement are the reality of many health, education, and other human service settings. The wind tunnel (see Stigler & Givvin, Chapter 6) is not a "hothouse" that perfects an entire intervention and then provides it wholesale to teachers to implement as an evidence-based practice. The cross-sector community initiative described in Chapter 3 uses a "lead user" approach to learn first within willing and able settings and then use this learning to introduce the same or adapted improvements to more challenged settings.

Professional Development in Improvement Science

Improvement science crosses boundaries of and integrates evaluative, innovation, and change management approaches. Optimal use of improvement science requires professionals who are skilled in improvement science and a ready system with a learning culture. Health care and now education and other sectors have burgeoning efforts to train improvement professionals and also prepare people within human service systems to succeed with the basics of improvement (Institute for Healthcare Improvement, 2003).

The chapters in this volume illustrate what is needed to advance improvement science within the evaluation profession. There is a need for training and professional development for those entering the field and for those in practice. What does improvement science add, how does the approach fit with evaluative approaches, and how can we reconcile the action orientation of improvement science with evaluative methods? Evaluation professionals need to be clear about the extent to which improvement science and evaluative approaches are derived from the same standards of establishing degree of belief and causality, as well as where improvement science is different from and challenges some commonly held practices in evaluation. In some cases, we need to confront what has been a main use of evaluative and applied research practice—that is, large-scale impact studies.

Moreover, there is a need to equip people with skills for learning and improvement that should be practiced at all levels of the system or organization, not just professional evaluators. In other words, for improvement science to succeed in evaluation, we need to build the capacity of stakeholders to think "evaluatively" (Schwandt, 2015). It is critical that we recognize that the culture of improvement through systematic investigation is still evolving within organizations and sectors and that professional evaluators can advance progress by promoting the methods. Systemic studies of what makes organizations succeed suggest that the "secret sauce" is a learning capability with ownership of improvement processes distributed across all levels of an organization and with leadership that focuses more on learning than on decision making (Spear, 2010).

New Directions for Evaluation • DOI: 10.1002/ev

Opportunities and Challenges

Many pressing societal problems demand more effective ways of developing concepts, trying them out under the range of relevant conditions, taking what works to scale, and spreading and sustaining them. The chapters in this volume make a case for the importance of understanding exactly what works, why, and how. Evaluators seek approaches that will yield "system solutions" rather than "hothouse" strategies that work only in limited or controlled settings. To be more successful with spread, there is interest in evaluative methods that generate learning that enables others to adopt what has been found to work. Practitioners are not well served by evaluations that underspecify changes (putting forth broad concepts that organizations are unable to translate into concrete actions) or that overspecify changes (producing fixed protocols that do not customize to fit all of the conditions of practice in the system). Growing interest of government, philanthropic organizations, and localities in producing collective impact in complex systems has created a demand for evaluation designs that would tell us what works, why it works, and how to apply what we know across all places and under all local conditions. The focus on systems is an opportunity for the evaluation field to respond with methods that fit the problem. We can respond with approaches that help people learn and innovate in that space.

The evaluation field is also looking for better ways of handling context. The conditions under which a theory and specific intervention works is always front and center. Transparency about context helps us to understand the relationship of cause and effect. When improvement science is applied to a localized problem, then the testing is limited to those local conditions. When it is applied with the intent of spreading beyond those local conditions, using planned experimentation (Moen et al., 2012), the implementation context for future spread is explicit and iterative testing is used to strengthen degree of belief about implementation in that context. The examples in this volume use improvement science as a method for ongoing learning that many human service systems need to make interventions work under varied and changing conditions.

The chapters also highlight challenges of improvement science. Many are familiar to evaluators. These include bringing people together across sectors to ask and answer questions, building relationships, establishing a common language, establishing shared goals, and cultivating skills of working professionals in measurement, testing, and action. An overarching challenge is readying systems to use the method. It means infusing a learning culture into organizations and systems, and setting aside the time and resources necessary for improvement to take place. As with some but not all evaluative approaches, improvement science is done "by" or "with" rather than "for," and there is no way around investing the time and space for reflection, learning, and action that it takes to craft changes that will work in practice.

To be sure, there are limitations to using improvement science as an evaluation approach. Rohanna (Chapter 5) and Stigler and Givvin (Chapter 6) describe the processes for implementing improvement science in educational settings. In educational evaluation, we often promise that we will produce instrumental, actionable information for the improvement of practices, which are in turn intended to produce better student outcomes. Most school administrators and teachers support processes that lead to these kinds of practice improvements. However, iterative learning inquiries require a sustained and prolonged commitment to the process of developing or adapting practice changes. Schools and community-based agencies are not research laboratories. There can be a fine line between doing research and evaluation; improvement science applies to both so it is critical that if we use improvement science for evaluative purposes, that we define the "evaluative space" of the work, and be aware if and when the work might slide into a space that is more characteristic of a research study. The balance between local learning and generalizable knowledge is also a longstanding critique of evaluation (Shadish, Cook, & Leviton, 1991) and so we see that both evaluation and improvement science share the concern for, and at times the struggle to maintain, the instrumental focus of the inquiry.

A major challenge is that a learning system requires data, organization, and human resources (Langley et al., 2009; Spear, 2010). These generally include and extend beyond the resources of conventional evaluation. The role of a skilled improvement coach (Ho, 2016) is not unlike that of the evaluator in a participatory evaluative process, where the coach helps to shape and implement the inquiry. This necessitates the training of both the practitioners and the coach or evaluator in improvement methods and evaluative processes, which takes time and can be costly. For improvement processes to sustain over time, practitioners need to integrate the role of learner in their professional identities (Ho, 2016). Healthcare and education professionals have a culture of autonomy that can be skeptical of shared learning processes. For practitioners and for evaluators, identity transformation is a dynamic process, which requires critical reflection and can trigger anxiety, apprehension, and unease (Snyder, Oliveira, & Paska, 2013). Because this work is highly collaborative, it requires facilitative and management skills (such as flexibility and communication) that take time to develop (Schwandt, 2015). And although collaborative inquiry processes can be empowering for practitioners, if not well balanced in the context of other work demands, they can be perceived as burdensome.

Health care and education are recognizing both the value of and the transformation needed to become learning systems that embed empiricism (local learning for improvement, and discovery that yields generalizable information) into daily work and management (Bryk, Gomez, Grunow, & LeMahieu, 2015; Institute of Medicine, 2013; Spear, 2010). Health care has embraced the learning health system model, which integrates discovery into care processes, as essential for improving value and outcomes (Institute of

Medicine, 2013; Seid, Margolis, & Opipari-Arrigan, 2014). This model is evolving in education as well (Bryk et al., 2015). Organizations and delivery systems will need to transform to make use of this method (Spear, 2010). The challenges described in these chapters illustrate some of the substantial mindset, skill, and resource requirements of integrating improvement science into a system of health care, education, or other human services.

Conclusion

There is great demand for approaches that accelerate learning and change in complex systems. Improvement science offers a system of learning—ways of testing, scaling, and spreading what is found to work—that achieves our ultimate goal, which is strategies that can sustain over time because they have been designed to do so under relevant conditions. This issue of *New Directions for Evaluation* offers several examples of how improvement science applied by people in the systems of interest can reach that goal. Although the chapters in this volume do not offer all of the answers, they offer examples of improvement science applied to problems of concern to evaluators in real-world systems such as health care, education, and cross-sector human development.

References

Bryk, A. S., Gomez, L. M., Grunow, A., & LeMahieu, P. G. (2015). *Learning to improve: How America's schools can get better at getting better*. Cambridge, MA: Harvard Education Press.

Deming, W. E. (2000). *Out of the crisis*. Boston, MA: MIT Press.

Gharajedaghi, J. (2011). *Systems thinking: managing chaos and complexity: A platform for designing business architecture* (3rd ed.). Burlington, MA: Elsevier.

Ho, J. (2016). *Cultures and contexts of data-based decision-making in schools* (Unpublished doctoral dissertation). University of California, Los Angeles.

Institute for Healthcare Improvement. (2003). *The Breakthrough Series: IHI's collaborative model for achieving breakthrough improvement*. IHI Innovation Series white paper. Boston, MA: Institute for Healthcare Improvement.

Institute of Medicine. (2013). *Best care at lower cost: The path to continuously learning health care in America*. Washington, DC: National Academies Press.

Langley, G. J., Moen, R. D., Nolan, K. M., Nolan, T. W., Norman, C. L., & Provost, L. P. (2009). *The improvement guide* (2nd ed.). San Francisco, CA: Jossey-Bass.

Massoud, M. R., Nielsen, G. A., Nolan, K., Nolan, T., Schall, M. W., & Sevin, C. (2006). *A framework for spread: From local improvements to system-wide change*. IHI Innovation Series white paper. Cambridge, MA: Institute for Healthcare Improvement.

Meadows, D. (2008). *Thinking in systems: A primer*. White River Junction, VT: Chelsea Green Publishing Company.

Moen, R. (2002). *A Guide to Idealized Design*. Cambridge, MA: Institute for Healthcare Improvement.

Moen, R. D., Nolan, T. W., & Provost, L. P. (2012). *Quality improvement through planned experimentation*. New York, NY: McGraw Hill.

Schwandt, T. (2015). *Evaluation foundations revisited: Cultivating a life of the mind for practice*. Stanford, CA: Stanford University Press.

Scoville, R., Little, K., Rakover, J., Luther, K., & Mate, K. (2016). *Sustaining improvement. IHI white paper*. Boston, MA: Institute for Healthcare Improvement.

Seid, M., Margolis, P. A., & Opipari-Arrigan, L. (2014). Engagement, peer production, and the learning healthcare system. *JAMA Pediatrics, 168*(3), 201–202.

Shadish, W., Cook, T., & Leviton, L. (1991). *Foundations of evaluation theory*. Thousand Oaks, CA: Sage.

Snyder, C., Oliveira, A. W., & Paska, L. M. (2013). STEM career changers' transformation into science teachers. *Journal of Science Teacher Education, 24*(4), 617–644.

Spear, S. J. (2010). *The high-velocity edge*. New York, NY: McGraw-Hill Education.

Weiss, C. H. (2010). *Scaling impact. Evaluation Exchange, XV(1)*. Boston, MA: Author. Retrieved from http://www.hfrp.org/evaluation/the-evaluation-exchange/issue-archive/current-issue-scaling-impact

MOIRA INKELAS is associate professor in the Department of Health Policy and Management in the Fielding School of Public Health, University of California, Los Angeles, and assistant director of the Center for Healthier Children, Families and Communities.

CHRISTINA A. CHRISTIE is professor and chair of the Department of Education in the Graduate School of Education and Information Studies, University of California, Los Angeles.

SEBASTIAN LEMIRE is a doctoral candidate in the Social Research Methodology Division in the Graduate School of Education and Information Studies, University of California, Los Angeles.

Index

103

NEW DIRECTIONS FOR EVALUATION

ORDER FORM SUBSCRIPTION AND SINGLE ISSUES

DISCOUNTED BACK ISSUES:

Use this form to receive 20% off all back issues of *New Directions for Evaluation*.
All single issues priced at **$23.20** (normally $29.00)

TITLE   ISSUE NO.   ISBN

_____ _____ _____

_____ _____ _____

Call 1-800-835-6770 or see mailing instructions below. When calling, mention the promotional code JBNND to receive your discount. For a complete list of issues, please visit www.wiley.com/WileyCDA/WileyTitle/productCd-EV.html

SUBSCRIPTIONS: (1 YEAR, 4 ISSUES)

☐ New Order   ☐ Renewal

U.S.	☐ Individual: $89	☐ Institutional: $380
CANADA/MEXICO	☐ Individual: $89	☐ Institutional: $422
ALL OTHERS	☐ Individual: $113	☐ Institutional: $458

Call 1-800-835-6770 or see mailing and pricing instructions below.
Online subscriptions are available at www.onlinelibrary.wiley.com

ORDER TOTALS:

Issue / Subscription Amount: $ _____

Shipping Amount: $ _____
(for single issues only – subscription prices include shipping)

Total Amount: $ _____

SHIPPING CHARGES:

First Item	$6.00
Each Add'l Item	$2.00

(No sales tax for U.S. subscriptions. Canadian residents, add GST for subscription orders. Individual rate subscriptions must be paid by personal check or credit card. Individual rate subscriptions may not be resold as library copies.)

BILLING & SHIPPING INFORMATION:

☐ **PAYMENT ENCLOSED:** *(U.S. check or money order only. All payments must be in U.S. dollars.)*

☐ **CREDIT CARD:** ☐ VISA   ☐ MC   ☐ AMEX

Card number _____ Exp. Date _____

Card Holder Name _____ Card Issue # _____

Signature _____ Day Phone _____

☐ **BILL ME:** *(U.S. institutional orders only. Purchase order required.)*

Purchase order # _____
           Federal Tax ID 13559302 • GST 89102-8052

Name _____

Address _____

Phone _____ E-mail _____

Copy or detach page and send to: **John Wiley & Sons, Inc. / Jossey Bass**
                                  PO Box 55381
                                  Boston, MA 02205-9850

PROMO JBNND